Ontario Birds

Ontario Birds

Chris Fisher

First printed in 1996 5 4 3

The Publisher
Lone Pine Publishing

206, 10426-81 Avenue
Edmonton, Alberta
Canada T6E 1X5

202A, 1110 Seymour Street
Vancouver, British Columbia
Canada V6B 3N3

1901 Raymond Ave S.W., Suite
Renton, Washington
U.S.A. 98055

Canadian Cataloguing in Publication Data
Fisher, Chris
Ontario birds

Includes bibliographical references and index.
ISBN 1-55105-069-2

1. Birds—Ontario—Identification. 2. Bird watching—Ontario. I. Title.
QL685.5.06F57 1996 598.29713 C96-910117-1

Technical Reviewer: David R.C. Prescott, Ph.D
Senior Editor: Nancy Foulds
Project Editor: Jennifer Keane
Design & Layout: Bruce Timothy Keith, Gregory Brown, Carol S. Dragich
Cover Design: Carol S. Dragich
Colour Illustrations: Gary Ross, Ewa Pluciennik, Horst Krause, Joan Johnston, Kitty Ho
Separations and Film: Elite Lithographers Co. Ltd., Edmonton, Alberta
Printing: Quality Color Press Inc., Edmonton, Alberta

The Publisher gratefully acknowledges the support of Alberta Community Development and the Canada/Alberta agreement on the cultural industries.

Illustration Credits

Gary Ross: 21, 22, 23, 26, 29, 30, 31, 35, 36, 38, 39, 40, 41, 44, 45, 46, 48, 50, 53, 57, 59, 60, 61, 62, 64, 68, 71, 72, 77, 80, 85, 87, 88, 91, 92, 93, 95, 97, 99, 101, 103, 104, 107, 109, 112, 114, 116, 120, 127, 130, 141, 144, cover

Ewa Pluciennik: 25, 33, 34, 37, 42, 43, 47, 49, 52, 54, 55, 56, 58, 63, 65, 67, 69, 73, 75, 76, 79, 81, 84, 89, 90, 94, 96, 98, 110, 113, 118, 119, 121, 122, 123, 125, 128, 133, 135, 136, 139, 140, 143

Horst Krause: 27, 28, 32, 51, 66, 86, 100, 105, 106, 108, 126

Joan Johnston: 70, 74, 83, 129, 131, 137, 146

Kitty Ho: 111

TABLE OF CONTENTS

ACKNOWLEDGEMENTS

A book such as this is made possible by the inspired work of Ontario's naturalists past and present. Their contributions continue to advance the science of ornithology and to motivate a new generation of nature lovers. My thanks to Gary Ross and Ewa Pluciennik, whose illustrations have elevated the quality of this book. Thanks to Carole Patterson for her continual support, and to Robin Bovey and Gerald McKeating, whose works served as models of excellence. Many thanks to the team at Lone Pine Publishing—Shane Kennedy, Jennifer Keane, Bruce Keith, and Nancy Foulds—for their input and steering. Jim Butler, Isabelle Richardson, Gord Court, Terry Thormin, and John Acorn all gave freely of their time to answer pesky little questions. Finally, my sincere thanks to Dr. David Prescott for reviewing the text and lending his expertise and patience to this project.

DEDICATION

To Gerard and Léa Fisher, whose patience, guidance, and support have enabled their son to share his passion with others.

INTRODUCTION

No matter where we live, birds are a natural part of our lives. We are so used to seeing them that we often take their presence for granted. When we take the time to notice their colours, songs, and behaviours, we see how dynamic these creatures are.

This book presents a brief introduction into the lives of birds. It is intended to serve as a bird identification guide, and also as a bird appreciation guide. Getting to know a bird's name is the first step toward getting to know birds. Once we've made contact with a species, we can better appreciate its character and mannerisms during future encounters. Over a lifetime of meetings, many birds become acquaintances, some seen daily, others not for years. When we know a bit about them, their songs will sound sweeter, their plumage will look brighter, and their hardships will no longer be discounted out of ignorance.

The selection of species within this book represents a balance between the familiar and the noteworthy. Many of the 126 species described in this guide are the most common species found in south and central Ontario; some are less common. It would be impossible for a beginner's book such as this to comprehensively describe all the birds found throughout the province of Ontario. The birds' natural abundance and distribution patterns ensure that sightings will vary considerably from place to place. There is no one site where all the species within this book can be observed simultaneously, but most species can be viewed—at least seasonally—within a few hours' drive of most cities and towns in southern Ontario.

The real story of birds unfolds outdoors. It is hoped that this guide will inspire novice birdwatchers into spending some time outdoors, gaining valuable experience with the local bird community. This book stresses the identity of birds, but it also attempts to bring them to life by discussing their various character traits, and interesting facts from the field of ornithology. We often discuss a bird's character traits in human terms, because personifying a bird's character can help us to feel a bond with the birds. These associations contribute greatly to the introduction of birds, but it is vital to realize that when we personify the actions of birds we satisfy our biased imaginations, but we do not do justice to the bird's complex behaviours.

FEATURES OF THE LANDSCAPE

Knowing where you are looking often reduces the confusion of what you are looking at. Because you won't find a grouse on a lake or a loon in a tree, habitat is important to note when birdwatching.

The quality of habitat is one of the most powerful factors to influence bird distribution, and with experience you may become amazed at the predictability of some birds within a specific habitat type. Just as humans have created environments that meet their needs, so birds are confined to environments that provide them with food and shelter. Within each bird description the bird's specific habitat is described. In most cases these habitat references complement the identification of the birds, but it is important to realize that because of their migratory habits, birds are sometimes found in completely different habitats outside of the breeding season.

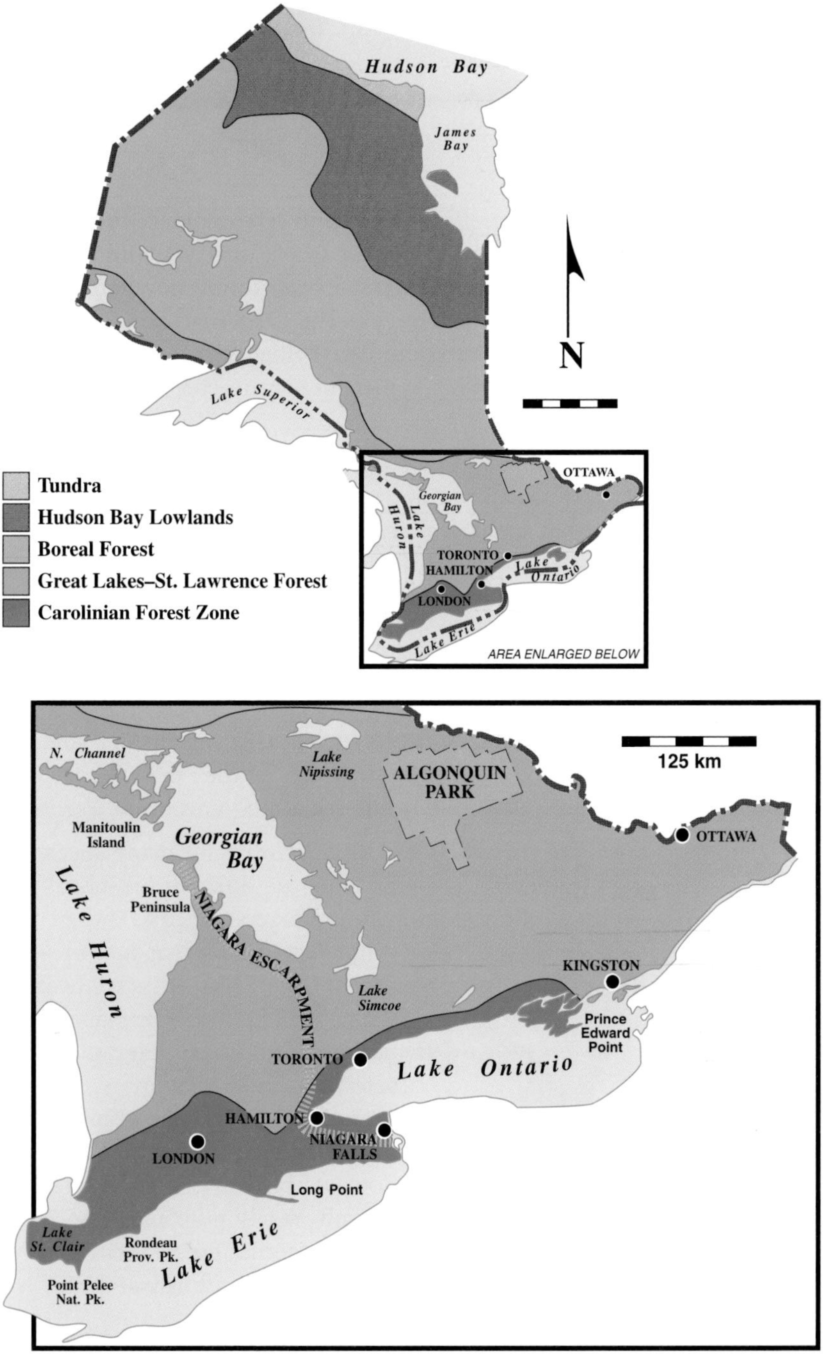

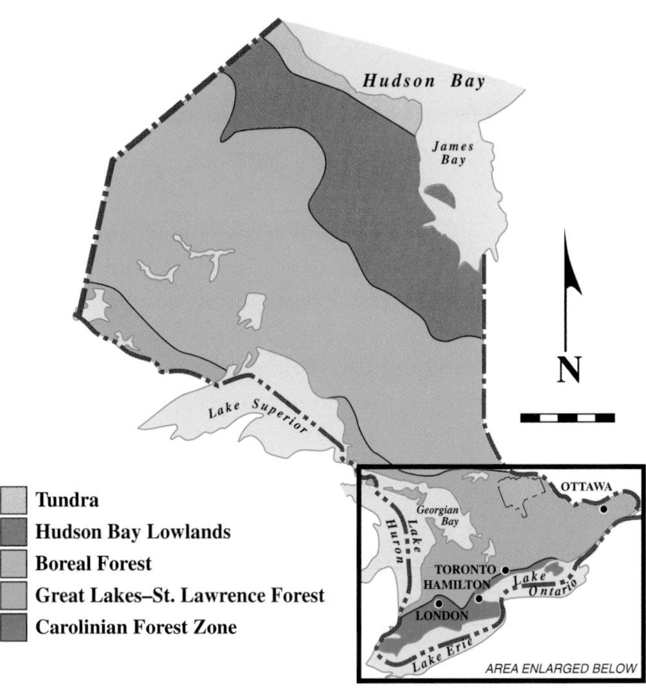
Hudson Bay
James Bay
N
Lake Superior
Tundra
Hudson Bay Lowlands
Boreal Forest
Great Lakes–St. Lawrence Forest
Carolinian Forest Zone
OTTAWA
Georgian Bay
Lake Huron
TORONTO
HAMILTON
Lake Ontario
LONDON
Lake Erie
AREA ENLARGED BELOW

N. Channel
Lake Nipissing
ALGONQUIN PARK
125 km
Manitoulin Island
Georgian Bay
OTTAWA
Lake Huron
Bruce Peninsula
NIAGARA ESCARPMENT
KINGSTON
Lake Simcoe
Prince Edward Point
TORONTO
Lake Ontario
HAMILTON
NIAGARA FALLS
LONDON
Long Point
Lake St. Clair
Rondeau Prov. Pk.
Lake Erie
Point Pelee Nat. Pk.

Carolinian Forest Zone

The Carolinian Zone (known as the deciduous forest in the eastern U.S.) is characterized in Ontario by southern species at their northern limit. Tulip-trees, sassafras, and Kentucky coffee trees are characteristic of this forest, and tree species diversity is very high. These moist, broad-leaf forests lie in the mildest region of Ontario, where relatively mild winters and hot summers support many species found nowhere else in Canada. Restricted to a large degree to the Carolinian Zone are the Hooded Warbler, Carolina Wren, and Red-bellied Woodpecker—among a host of other birds more typical of southeastern U.S. forests.

Although this book doesn't attempt to cover this unique and threatened ecosystem, the Carolinian deserves at least a brief mention. The Carolinian Forest has all but disappeared in southern Ontario, and now occurs only in small, isolated plots. Many parks established to preserve the Carolinian along Lake Erie (Rondeau Provincial Park, Point Pelee National Park, Long Point) are also some of the few breeding areas in Canada for many songbirds. Because many of these birds are limited in Ontario, they are not reviewed in this book, although their occurrence is of considerable interest to Ontario naturalists.

It is hoped that introductory books such as this will inspire novice birdwatchers to expand their birding interests so they may choose to explore the vast natural potential in the remaining Carolinian Forests.

The southern tip of Ontario is like a giant funnel for many species of birds. The open waters of the Great Lakes are difficult for most birds to cross, so they follow shorelines and take shortcuts, flying across the shortest sections of open water. The points that jut out into the Great Lakes (Point Pelee, Rondeau, Long Point, Prince Edward Point) are like welcome mats for the tired and weary migrants. It is to these areas that an unsurpassed diversity of migrant birds flocks in the spring—with flocks of birdwatchers not far behind. Yearly pilgrimages to birding meccas are events all North American birdwatchers hope to experience.

Great Lakes-St. Lawrence Mixed Forest

This highly developed ecoregion is the area of focus for much of this book. As most Ontarians live within (or near) the Great Lakes-St. Lawrence Mixed Forest, it is the natural setting for a beginner's bird guide for Ontario. Historically, much of the area was covered by a continuous forest of mainly hardwood deciduous trees, which contributed to a rich bird life. Deforestation and agricultural development have reduced the continuous forests into small, isolated patches, although continuous stretches still remain around the Bruce Peninsula and around cottage country. The conversion of the landscape has had a serious impact on the bird life of the Great Lakes-St. Lawrence Mixed Forests, and birds associated with this forest structure have declined in step with the forests. For species like the Wood Thrush, the remaining large stands of forests in southern Ontario are but teasing reminders of the vast forested landscape that once covered the entire region.

Despite the decline of several forest birds, the bird life of southern Ontario has actually become more diverse because of the expansion of agriculture. In the past, few open fields occurred naturally, but now pastures and meadows are regular occurrences; these areas host breeding birds that formerly were scarce in this region. Upland Sandpipers, Eastern Meadowlarks, and other open-country dwellers have benefitted from the effects of agriculture, and have expanded their range into Ontario following the clearing of the forests.

Similarly, many species that prefer second-growth young forests, such as the Chestnut-sided Warbler, have become abundant in areas where they were previously seldom seen. Scattered abandoned farmlands and overgrown fields are slowly aging and leading patches of southern Ontario back to its forested past, providing a diverse landscape exploited by certain bird species. This area of the province also has many conifer plantations, which further add to the diversity of the landscape. The often small and isolated plantations have in turn attracted northern-nesting species to breed south of their expected range. Golden-crowned Kinglets and Red-breasted Nuthatches are now found in these artificial boreal environments, far from the traditional continuous coniferous woods.

The Great Lakes-St. Lawrence Mixed Forest will never again regain the species composition of pre-colonial times, and those areas remnant of natural forests are links to the province's treasured natural history. The bird species that have adapted to changes in the landscape and have invaded the province add to the wealth of Ontario's natural diversity.

Despite the transformation that has occurred within the Great Lakes-St. Lawrence Mixed Forests, many natural features remain. Of special concern to birders is the Niagara Escarpment, a huge limestone arc that slices through Ontario from the Bruce Peninsula to Niagara Falls. This limestone escarpment is heavily forested in places, providing a rich habitat for many songbirds. The Niagara Escarpment is also an interesting feature in raptor (and other bird) migration, as many birds trace their way across the province using the limestone belt as a highway.

Marshes concentrate birds both during migration and during the breeding season. Although many marshes have been drained, many still occur in southern Ontario, and bevies of birds can be encountered in those areas during the warm months. These habitats can be difficult to access, and some of the birds that are present are often secretive and difficult to observe.

During peak migratory periods, wetlands are excellent sites to observe birds. Favourite places to view waterfowl and shorebirds are not necessarily the pristine marshes—naturalists in Ontario are frequently rewarded with the sight of thousands of birds along the busy shorelines of the Great Lakes, and at sewage lagoons. As odd as it may seem, sewage lagoons offer some of the best birding in Ontario; they are nutrient-rich and easily accessible, they rarely freeze, and (believe it or not) our sense of smell usually becomes acclimatized to the pungent odour within a matter of minutes.

Boreal Forest

The Boreal Forest is one of the largest terrestrial ecosystems in the world and it covers much of northern Ontario. This dynamic region, dominated by spruce, birch, and aspen, dips into central Ontario near Lake Nipissing and Algonquin Provincial Park. Many migrants that pass through southern Ontario choose to nest in the Boreal Forest. The Great Lakes-St. Lawrence Mixed Forest around cottage country and the Bruce Peninsula have many boreal elements and share many species of breeding birds. Apart from being the breeding ground of many tropical migrants, the Boreal Forest is the breeding site of many species (such as Evening Grosbeaks, Purple Finches, and crossbills) that overwinter in southern Ontario. As these forests are increasingly commercialized and logged, the tropical migrant and winter finch populations that visit southern Ontario may be affected.

THE ORGANIZATION OF THIS BOOK

Most other field guides are directed toward accomplished birdwatchers who are capable of sorting out which of the 800 North American species occur in their region, in strict phylogenetic order. There is nothing wrong with many of these excellent guides, but they are very complex. Novice birdwatchers rarely have the five- or ten-minute view of a species that is required to search those large volumes. *Ontario Birds* groups birds by physical appearance and behaviour, without always adhering to the scientific criteria for bird classification. It is easier for a novice to associate a wren as a 'small songbird' than as a 'Troglodytidae.' It is hoped that this modified order will allow you to spend more time with the birds and less time fumbling through a field guide.

Diving Birds

loons, grebes, cormorants

These distinctive birds are adapted to dive for their food, and for that reason are most frequently seen on the surface of the water. All these birds are quite distinctive and can only be confused with one another or with certain waterfowl.

Wetland Waders

rails, herons

Although this group varies considerably in size and represents two separate groups of related birds, their habitat and food preferences are similar. Long-legged birds of marshes, the wetland waders are quite common, although certain species are seen far more frequently than are others.

Waterfowl

swans, geese, ducks

Swans, geese, and ducks represent a distinct group of birds. Although certain species differ in their feeding habits and bill characteristics, this group remains straightforward.

Hawks and Eagles

These daytime hunters are distinctive in spite of the various habitats they choose to occupy. From deep forests to open country to large lakes, there are hawks and eagles to hunt the skies. The predatory look of their sharp talons, hooked bills, and forward-facing eyes easily identifies this group.

Shorebirds

sandpipers, plovers

The sandpipers and plovers are not always confined to the shores of our lakes and marshes; some species choose to avoid the water altogether. Although most of our shorelines host the small, long-legged, swift-flying birds, don't be surprised to find some of these birds in pastures and open fields.

Gulls and Terns

Gulls are familiar to all, but terns are far less frequently seen. Terns are related to gulls but are smaller and far less likely to be seen on the ground.

Owls

The night hunters are seen silhouetted against the moonlit sky. Owls are enjoyed by many people, perhaps for the birds' human-like facial features. To overcome the difficulty in reliably seeing these night dwellers, learn their calls.

Ground Feeders

grouse, doves, larks

All birds in this group feed mostly on the ground, but so do many other birds in Ontario. Since all the others had many relatives with which to be grouped, these ground feeders were grouped together by feeding behaviour. While most of the birds in this group are familiar to the beginner, the smaller Horned Lark (which is frequently seen in open fields) behaves very much like a sparrow of the open country.

Aerial Feeders

nightjars, swifts, hummingbirds, kingfishers

This is a group of several small and unrelated families. The swift and the nightjars (nighthawk and Whip-poor-will) are usually seen flying about in open areas, catching insects on the wing. The swift is truly related to the hummingbird and is much smaller than the night-flying nightjars. The Belted Kingfisher is a distinctive bird that has no close relatives in Ontario; it is frequently seen perched or hovering above open water.

Woodpeckers

The drumming sound of wood being hammered and these birds' precarious foraging habits easily identify most members of this distinctive group. Even when these birds are not seen or heard, their characteristic marks can be seen on trees in any mature forest.

Flycatchers

flycatchers, phoebes, kingbirds

This distinctive family is perhaps best identified by foraging behaviour. As their name implies, flycatchers catch insects by darting after them from a favourite perch. Most flycatchers sing simple but distinctive songs.

Swallows

Members of this distinctive family are seen flying or at their nest site. Small but sleek, swallows fly gracefully in pursuit of insects. Whatever the habitat in southern Ontario, there is a swallow to match it.

Corvids

jays, crows, ravens

Many members of this family are familiar to Ontarians because of the intelligence and adaptability of this group of birds. These easily observed birds are often extremely bold, teasing the animal-human barrier.

Small Songbirds

chickadees, nuthatches, kinglets, wrens

These birds are grouped together on the basis of size and habitat. All are smaller than a sparrow and, with the exception of the Marsh Wren, are generally found in forested areas.

Thrushes

Beautiful singers, from the robin to the bluebird and the secretive forest thrushes, this group has the finest collective voice. Although some members of this group are very familiar, others are found only with experience and patience.

Forest Edge Birds

cuckoos, mimics, starlings, shrikes

These unrelated birds are generally all the same size—a bit smaller than a robin. Most of these birds are found in shrubby areas or along forest edges. Although a great many other birds also fall into this habitat, most are usually far smaller or larger.

Warblers and Vireos

This large and diverse group represents the warbler family and the vireo family. Ontario is blessed with many of these small, quick, and musical birds. They are very diverse in plumage, with some individuals splashed liberally with colours and others dressed in pale olive. Initial encounters with this group can be frustrating, but most experienced birders agree that warblers and vireos are the most rewarding birds to watch.

Colourful Songbirds

tanagers, cardinals, allies

This is another group tossed together not because of strict relation, but because of individual beauty. All birds within this group are sized between a sparrow and a robin, but the bird's dimensions are not what immediately strike the observer. Contrasting colours and vivid pigments set this group of songsters apart from others.

Blackbirds

blackbirds, meadowlarks, orioles

All birds in this family belong to the blackbird family. It may surprise beginners that the meadowlark, bobolink, and oriole are truly blackbirds, so it is hoped that this grouping reinforces the realization.

Sparrows

sparrows, buntings, juncos

These small, often indistinct, birds are predominantly brown or olive. Their songs are often very useful in identification. Many novice (and occasionally even experienced) birdwatchers discount many of these sparrows as simply little brown birds, unfortunate since these birds have characteristics worthy of the extra identification effort.

Finches

finches, grosbeaks, crossbills, redpolls

Many of these often colourful birds are most frequently seen during the winter as they spill out of the boreal forest or the tundra into southern Ontario. As many of the finches are birdfeeder regulars, these birds are familiar parts of the winter scene.

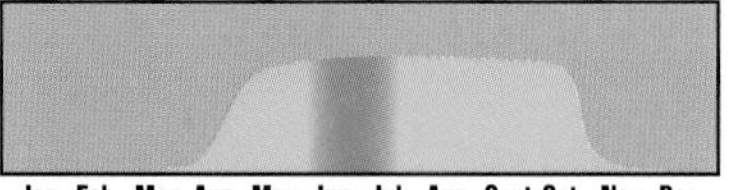

ABUNDANCY CHARTS

Accompanying each bird description is a chart that indicates the relative abundance of the species throughout the year in south and central Ontario. These stylized graphs offer some insight to the distribution and abundance of the birds, but they should not be viewed as definitive because there is much variation in bird behaviour.

Each chart is divided into 12 boxes, each box representing a month of the year. The pale orange that colours the chart is an indication of abundance; the more colour the more common the bird. The darker orange colour indicates the approximate nesting period. Where no dark orange colour is shown, no breeding records for that particular species occur in southern Ontario. Many species nest to the north and visit southern Ontario in significant numbers during migration or during the winter.

The graphs are based on personal observations and various excellent sources (Goodwin 1995, Peck and James 1983, Peck and James 1987, and Speirs 1985).

Absent

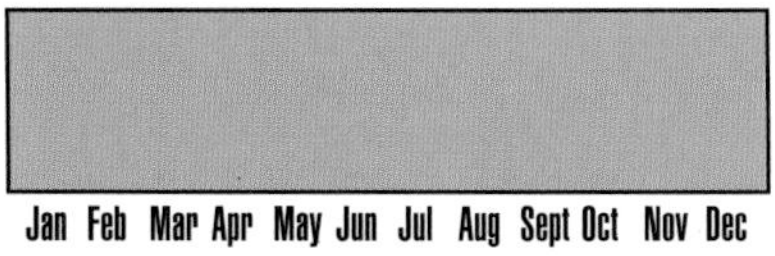

Jan Feb Mar Apr May Jun Jul Aug Sept Oct Nov Dec

Uncommon

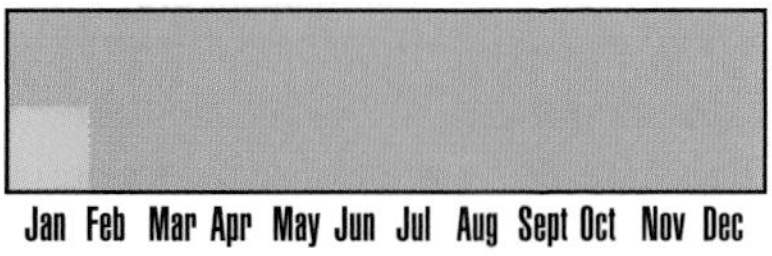

Jan Feb Mar Apr May Jun Jul Aug Sept Oct Nov Dec

Unlikely

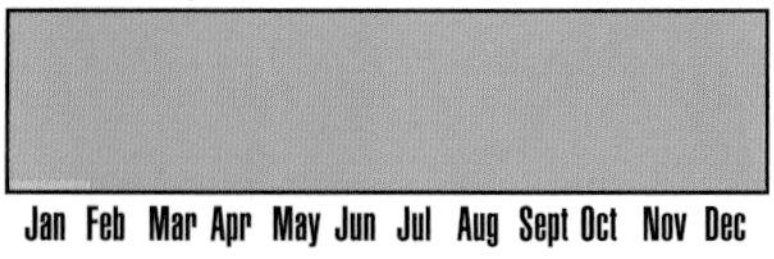

Jan Feb Mar Apr May Jun Jul Aug Sept Oct Nov Dec

Common

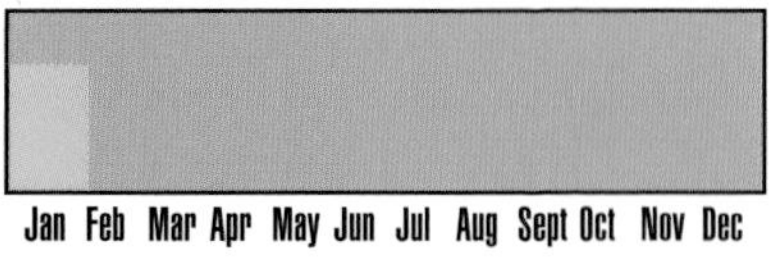

Jan Feb Mar Apr May Jun Jul Aug Sept Oct Nov Dec

Rare

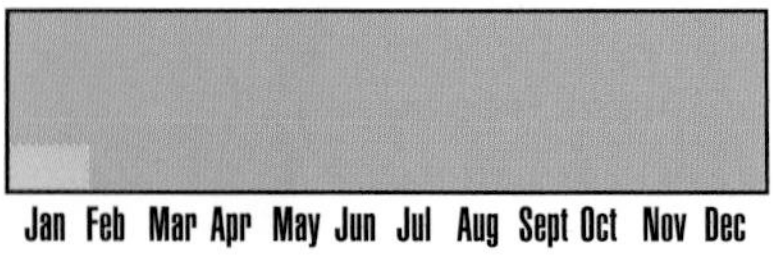

Jan Feb Mar Apr May Jun Jul Aug Sept Oct Nov Dec

Abundant

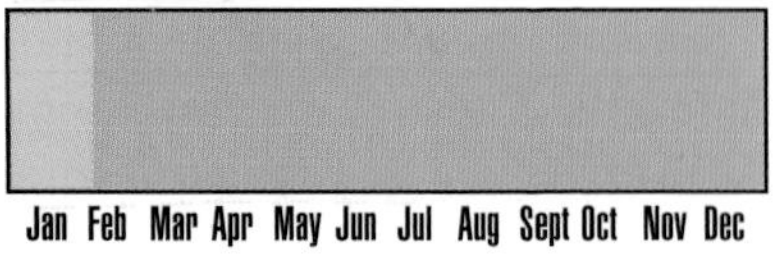

Jan Feb Mar Apr May Jun Jul Aug Sept Oct Nov Dec

Common Loon 

Gavia immer

THE CALL of the Common Loon sanctifies northern lakes with a primordial yodel. The invigorating song tingles the senses and refreshes a human soul soiled by traffic noises and urban sprawl. The presence of a pair reinforces the wilderness quality of the lake; Common Loons prefer areas without disruptive powerboats and shoreline development. With its intricate black and white plumage, dark green hood, and fine necklace, the loon is increasingly being used as a symbol of excellence and quality by marketing firms that recognize a valuable national treasure.

The loon is a noble symbol of northern wilderness, preferring the diminishing pristine areas where birds alone quarrel over naval rights of way. Spending time near a family of loons on a summer's evening, nature lovers can experience an intangible wilderness spirit in place, time, and circumstance.

Quick ID: larger than a duck; **breeding:** dark green hood; checkerboard black and white back; fine, white necklace; bill stout and sharp; hunchbacked in flight; **non-breeding:** sandy-brown back; light underparts; sexes similar.

Size: 82 cm (32 in.)

Habitat: large lakes; cottage country to northern Ontario.

Nest: mound of plants and mud; on undisturbed shoreline, vulnerable to human disturbances.

Food: small fish, aquatic insects, amphibians, crustaceans.

Foraging: pursues prey underwater to depths of 60 m.

Voice: alarm call 'tremelo' (both sexes); contact call 'wail' (both sexes); territorial call 'yodel' (males only); intimacy 'hoot' (both sexes).

Similar Species: Common Merganser (p. 38); Double-crested Cormorant (p. 23).

Notes: Because they have solid bones (unlike chickens and most other birds, which have hollow bones) and their legs are placed well back on their bodies for diving, Common Loons require long stretches of open water for take-off. Some loons are fatally trapped every year by constricting ice as lakes freeze in fall.

Pied-billed Grebe

Podilymbus podiceps

THE SMALL, SQUAT, DRAB BODY of the Pied-billed Grebe seems perfectly suited to its marshy habitat, but its loud whooping is strangely foreign. The distinctive *kuk-kuk-kuk-cow-cow-cow-cowp-cowp* sound seems more at home in tropical rainforests than murky cattail wetlands.

Pied-billed Grebes can be found—or at least heard—on most freshwater wetlands that are surrounded by emergent vegetation such as cattails and bulrushes. These small grebes are frustrating to follow as they appear and disappear effortlessly from the reedy margins of the marsh. Their perky foraging dives slice through the wetland surface, often without creating a ripple. Pied-billed Grebes lack the splendid plumage of many wetland birds, but there may be no other bird that is better suited to a marshy life.

Quick ID: pigeon-sized; **breeding:** all-brown; dark vertical band on laterally compressed bill; sexes similar; **Immatures:** striped.

Size: 33 cm (13 in.)

Habitat: marshes and weedy wetlands that provide cover.

Nest: grasses and weeds; often attached to floating plants, inconspicuous, hidden in emergent vegetation.

Food: small fish, aquatic invertebrates, amphibians, water plants.

Foraging: shallow dives, surface gleaning.

Voice: *kuk-kuk-kuk-cow-cow-cow-cowp-cowp-cowp.*

Similar Species: young ducks; Horned and Red-necked Grebes are larger, more colourful, and are uncommon in Ontario.

Notes: Unlike most other waterbirds, grebes do not have webbed feet. The toes of all grebes are broad and lobed, an adaptation to swimming. • The Pied-billed Grebe often eats discarded feathers, frequently packing its digestive system. It is thought that this behaviour may protect the stomach from sharp fish bones, and slow their passage through the digestive system so that nutrients are absorbed and not passed.

Double-crested Cormorant

Phalacrocorax auritus

THIS PREHISTORIC-LOOKING BIRD is Ontario's only cormorant and is commonly seen flying, single-file, low over open water. Somewhere in the evolutionary process, cormorants lost (or perhaps had never acquired) the ability to waterproof their wings, so they need to dry their wings after each swim. These large black waterbirds are frequently seen perched on bridge pilings, sand bars and buoys, with their wings partially spread, exposing their wet feathers to sun and wind. The cormorant's ability to wet its feathers decreases its buoyancy, making it easier for it to swim after the fish on which it preys.

Cormorants are one of the few birds that are best appreciated from a distance. Our overly sensitive sense of smell and biased perception of beauty don't promote many return trips to odoriferous cormorant colonies.

Quick ID: goose-sized black waterbird; long tail; long neck kinked in flight; rapid wingbeats; **breeding:** throat pouch more orange; streamy white eyebrow plumes (seen only at close range); sexes similar; **Immatures:** brown with a white belly.

Size: 81 cm (32 in.)

Habitat: large lakes, Great Lakes, cottage country.

Nest: made of sticks, aquatic vegetation, and guano; on low-lying islands or precariously high in trees.

Food: small to mid-sized fish, occasionally aquatic invertebrates.

Foraging: long underwater dives from the water's surface.

Voice: generally quiet, occasional grunts or croaks.

Similar Species: winter-plumage loons; large, dark ducks and geese are generally more squat.

Notes: Like their close relatives the pelicans, cormorants have a naked throat pouch and fully webbed feet (all four toes are linked with webbing). All black, and lacking sweat glands (only a few mammals sweat) Double-crested Cormorants can be seen with their bills open, panting to cool off. Sealed nostrils, a long, rudder-like tail, and excellent underwater vision also complement the Double-crested Cormorants' aquatic lifestyle.

American Bittern

Botaurus lentiginosus

PARTING CATTAILS OR BULRUSHES with a canoe frequently causes much distress to a variety of wetland birds that are associated with the emergent vegetation. An American Bittern will freeze at the slightest unwelcome sound, its bill pointing skyward to reveal the vertical chest streaks that blend with its cattail home. This defensive behaviour is so effective that the mid-sized bittern is frequently overlooked. Should the disruption persist, however, the bittern will fly off as a last resort, usually signalling its dismay with a 'whitewash salute' as it clears the cattail tops.

A spring evening is incomplete without the deep, funky call of an American Bittern echoing across a marsh. The hollow, rhythmic tones are often the only way to identify a bittern's presence, and they have inspired more than a few overwhelmed birders to perform a wetland jig.

Quick ID: hawk-sized; heavy brown vertical streaking; short tail; long legs; short, round wings; dagger-like bill; sexes similar.

Size: 60 cm (24 in.)

Habitat: cattail or bulrush marshes, tall, partially submerged vegetation.

Nest: simple grass or sedge construction; above the water line in tall vegetation, with separate entrance and exit paths.

Food: small fish, amphibians, small rodents, invertebrates.

Foraging: patient sit-and-wait, occasionally slow, purposeful stalking.

Voice: slow, resonant, repetitive *pomp-er-lunk*, most often heard at night.

Similar Species: Least Bittern is smaller; immature herons lack heavy chest streaking.

Notes: Lost or migrating American Bitterns are sometimes seen in unusual places. Whether they are encountered in trees, fields, or beaches, they instinctively freeze, despite a lack of concealing vegetation. American Bitterns always freeze facing intruders, and will turn should the disturbance circle them.

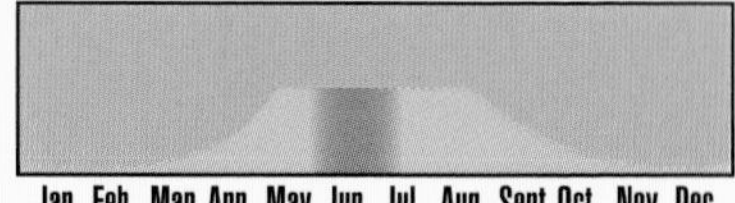

Great Blue Heron

Ardea herodias

THE GREAT BLUE HERON is one of the largest birds in Ontario. It often stands motionless as it surveys the calm waters, its graceful lines blending naturally with the dancing grasses and cattails of wetlands, or the breaking waves of the Great Lakes.

This great sentry is familiar to most Ontario residents—its large size and regal appearance are difficult to overlook. During breeding season, majestic plumes stream from this heron's head and throat, adding to the bird's elegance. A metaphor of patience, a hunting heron will not strike out with its cocked bill until it can be assured of a meal. In flight, Great Blue Herons are just as laid back, their lazy wingbeats slowly but effortlessly carrying them up to their nests.

Quick ID: very large; grey-blue plumage; red thighs; long, dagger-like yellow bill; head folded back and legs held straight back in flight; sexes similar.

Size: 125 cm (45 in.)

Habitat: wetlands, lakes, streams, and rivers, with nearby woodlands.

Nest: flimsy, bulky mass of sticks; high in trees, often in colonies.

Food: small to mid-sized fish, amphibians, small mammals, even carrion.

Foraging: stand-and-wait predator, strikes at prey with speed and power.

Voice: *frahnk frahnk frahnk*, deep and harsh.

Similar Species: Sandhill Crane flies with its neck outstretched, migrates through southern Ontario.

Notes: Many long-necked birds fly with neck extended, but herons have a specialized vertebrae that enables their neck to fold back over itself. The S-shaped neck is a useful field mark for many herons.

Green Heron

Butorides virescens

THIS CROW-SIZED HERON is far less conspicuous than its Great Blue cousin. The Green Heron prefers to hunt for frogs and small fish in shallow, weedy wetlands—a habit that likely leads to low estimates of its abundance.

The Green Heron often uses all of its tiny stature to hunt over a favourite site. With its bright yellow feet clasping a branch or reed, this small heron stretches nearly horizontal over water until it is satisfied that a fish will soon appear. Its patient concentration is unbroken and its pose rigid and unchanging until an ill-fated fish swims into range. Like a taut bowstring, the heron tenses before it fires. Lunging its entire body at its prey, the small heron is often soaked to the shoulders following a successful hunt. Inconspicuous and beautiful, this bird occurs commonly throughout southern Ontario wetlands, but it treats few birdwatchers to the sight of its dynamic hunting style.

Quick ID: crow-sized, stubby heron; short legs; glossy green back; chestnut throat; dark cap; sexes similar but male's colour and plumes more intense during breeding; **Immatures:** less colourful, with more streaking.

Size: 47 cm (19 in.)

Habitat: marshes and brushy wetlands, including lakes, streams, and swamps.

Nest: interwoven twigs and sticks; often in trees, shrubs, or dense shoreline vegetation.

Food: fish, amphibians, aquatic invertebrates.

Foraging: slowly stalks prey in dense vegetation or crouches to sit and wait.

Voice: loud, unexpected *kyowk*.

Similar Species: other herons; American Bittern (p. 24); Least Bittern; all lack a green back.

Notes: When plumes were highly prized clothing accessories earlier this century, heron plumes were the most sought-after. Breeding male herons are adorned with several long, graceful feathers that stream from their heads and necks. Although the plumes of the Green Heron were not as prized as those from some of its close relatives, many of these small herons paid a high price for fashion.

Jan Feb Mar Apr May Jun Jul Aug Sept Oct Nov Dec

Virginia Rail

Rallus limicola

RAILS ARE MYSTERIOUS BIRDS. They have secretive habits and unwelcoming homes, and while most people are unaware they exist, devout birdwatchers go to ridiculous efforts to see them.

Urban sprawl and agricultural expansion, which have drained many marshes, have come at the expense of many Ontario birds. The Virginia Rail's marshland habitat is often thought to be unproductive by human standards, but these shallow, nutrient-rich wetlands host a bounty of wildlife. With the growing legion of birdwatchers and nature lovers, societal values are continually shifting toward a holistic understanding of our natural communities.

Quick ID: robin-sized; cinnamon breast; large feet; long, reddish bill; sexes similar.

Size: 24 cm (10 in.)

Habitat: cattail marshes, dense wet meadows.

Nest: suspended over mud or water; basket woven with vegetation and lined with grass.

Food: aquatic invertebrates, often snails.

Foraging: gleans partially submerged vegetation and substrate.

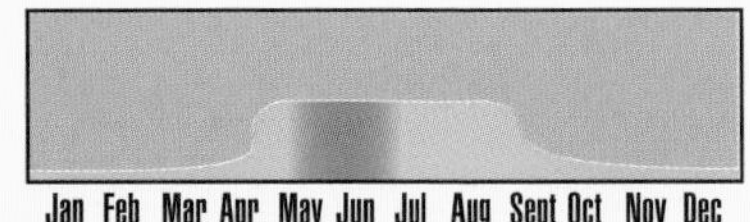

Voice: descending *wak-wak-wak-wak-wak.*

Similar Species: Sora has a black mask, dark body, and short bill; Pied-billed Grebe (p. 22) has a short bill; American Bittern (p. 24) is much larger, with a longer bill; Marsh Wren (p. 97) is smaller, with a cocked-up tail.

Notes: Rails in Ontario can best be identified by sound. The Yellow Rail sounds like two stones striking together—*tick tick, tick tick tick, tick tick, tick tick tick*—while the eerie call of the Sora—*So-Ra, So-Ra, weeweeweewee-wee-wee-wee*—descends characteristically at the end. The expression 'thin as a rail' refers to these laterally thin birds, which must squeeze through the tight confines of cattail marshes.

Common Moorhen
Gallinula chloropus

THE COMMON MOORHEN is a curious mix of comedy and confusion: it appears to have been made from bits and pieces left over from other birds. Its bill is chicken-like and its oversized feet would look more natural under a heron. Despite not having any webbing on its toes, the Common Moorhen insists on swimming, an indication that it must have the swimming instinct of a duck. It is a credit to nature's mystery that, despite its gangly appearance, the Common Moorhen is a successful inhabitant of many Ontario marshes.

Although the Common Moorhen looks awkward, its careful paces are executed with amazing grace. As the Common Moorhen commutes around its wetland home, its head mirrors the actions of its legs. As it steps, its head bobs back and forth in perfect synchrony, resulting in a comical, chugging stride.

Quick ID: larger than a pigeon; slate-black chest, neck, and head; red bill tipped with yellow; long, cumbersome toes; white horizontal line high on flanks; sexes similar.

Size: 36 cm (14 in.)

Habitat: deep-water marshes, cattail wetlands.

Nest: cup nest made of aquatic plants, occasionally has a roof; built over water.

Food: aquatic vegetation, some aquatic invertebrates.

Foraging: surface feeds, gleans off water, occasionally dabbles.

Voice: high-pitched *kr-r-rruk, kek, kek, kek, kek.*

Similar Species: American Coot has an all-white bill; ducks and grebes all lack red bill.

Notes: Common Moorhens are most closely related to the rails, coots, and cranes. The American Coot is a common neighbour of the Moorhen. The American Coot's stout white bill, all-black body, and cranky disposition help to distinguish it from the ducks with which it associates. • The Common Moorhen was formerly known as the 'Common Gallinule.'

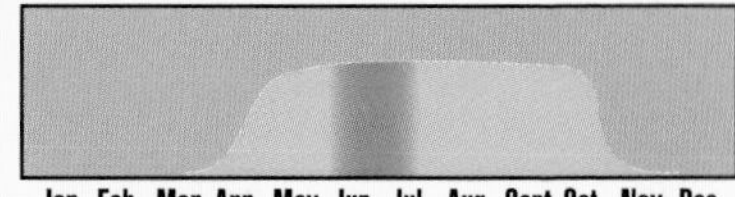

Trumpeter Swan
Cygnus buccinator

ONCE VALUED FOR ITS great feathers, soft skin, and tasty meat, the magnificent Trumpeter Swan is slowly regaining the range it lost shortly after European colonization. The Ontario population of this great bird was one of the early casualties of settlement, and healthy populations of Trumpeter Swans now occur only in the West. It is hoped that reintroduction into suitable habitats will succeed so that Ontario residents of the 21st century will be able to know the largest North American waterfowl for its grace and its intrinsic contributions to the landscape.

Two swans more commonly seen in Ontario are the Trumpeter's close relative the Tundra Swan, and the introduced Mute Swan. The Tundra Swan migrates through Ontario between its Arctic breeding grounds and its American wintering habitat. The graceful Mute Swan is now established around some urban areas.

Quick ID: very large; black bill, legs, and eyes; otherwise all white; no black in the wings; generally holds neck straight while swimming; sexes similar.

Size: 152 cm (60 in.)

Habitat: reintroduced; large wetlands, marshes, lakes.

Nest: large mound of vegetation and mud; in water.

Food: aquatic vegetation, roots and tubers, eats waste grain while migrating.

Foraging: probes and uproots vegetation on shorelines, while swimming frequently 'tips up' in shallow water, probing the lake bed by extending its long neck down while keeping its body on the surface.

Voice: deep and resonant *koo-hoh.*

Similar Species: Tundra Swan has a small yellow teardrop; Mute Swan has an orange bill with a black knob.

Notes: This swan's loud call is responsible for both its common and scientific species name: *buccinator* means 'one who trumpets,' while *cygnus* simply means 'swan.' The bird's long windpipe loops through its sternum, and the extra length amplifies its powerful voice.

Canada Goose
Branta canadensis

LIKE LEAVES ON TREES, Canada Geese are indicators of changing seasons. Their magnificent spring and autumn migrations now touch many Ontario residents, but less than a century ago, the sight of a large flock of Canada Geese was rare in Ontario. Much of the turnaround in the population of these magnificent birds can be attributed to Ontario's own Jack Miner. Wild Goose Jack fed many geese, banded many, and most importantly, increased awareness toward conservation. Today's Canada Geese, now commonly seen in city parks and wetland marshes, are a reminder of heroic early conservation efforts by concerned naturalists like Jack Miner.

Breeding pairs are regal in appearance and are legendarily loyal. They mate for life, and not only will a widowed goose occasionally remain unpaired for the rest of its life, it's also common for a mate to remain at the side of a fallen partner.

Quick ID: large, wild goose; white cheek; black head and neck; brown body; white undertail coverts; sexes similar.

Size: 110 cm (43 in.)

Habitat: widespread in city parks, golf courses, agricultural fields, small wetlands.

Nest: raised mound of vegetation and mud usually near, but occasionally far from, water.

Food: aquatic vegetation, roots and tubers, grasses, waste grain.

Foraging: often grazes on land, also feeds by tipping up from the water's surface.

Voice: loud and characteristic *ah-honk*.

Similar Species: other large, dark-coloured waterfowl.

Notes: Although Canada Geese are common throughout southern Ontario, all flocks are not the same. Many subspecies migrate through Ontario, and can be recognized by the differences in size. In general, the further north the geese are heading, the smaller they will be, and the largest geese found in Ontario are often those that migrate little, if at all.

Wood Duck

Aix sponsa

ONLY DAYS OLD, small Wood Duck chicks are lured out of the only world they know by their pleading mother. Although this seems typical of most ducks, young Wood Ducks require more coaxing than most—their nest is an old woodpecker hole high in a tree. With a faith-filled leap, the cottonball ducklings tumble toward the ground, often bouncing on impact. When all the siblings have leapt into the waiting world, they follow their mother through the dense underbrush to the nearest water.

Many of the old, rotten, hollow lakeside trees that provided excellent nesting sites for Wood Ducks have been removed from southern Ontario. As a result, more and more young Wood Ducks are beginning life by tumbling out of human-made nest boxes. These nesting programs have benefits for all parties involved. The Wood Ducks are provided with a secure nest site in which to incubate their eggs, while landowners have the honour of having North America's most handsome duck living on their land.

Quick ID: small duck; **Male:** elegant plumage; crested green head streaked with white; white throat; chestnut breast; white shoulder slash; **Female:** large, white teardrop; small crest; yellow legs; fine, white breast streaks.

Size: 47 cm (18 in.)

Habitat: woodland lakes, beaver ponds, streams.

Nest: often near water, in woodpecker holes, nest boxes, or hollow trunks; lined with down and wood chips.

Food: seeds, berries, grains, invertebrates.

Foraging: grazing, dabbling, tipping up.

Voice: squeaky *oo-eek oo-eek oo-eek.*

Similar Species: female Wood Ducks resemble many other small hens; males are very distinctive.

Notes: The male Wood Duck is undoubtedly the most elegant North American duck. Its image graces more book covers, calendars, and magazines than any other waterfowl. Having such a celebrity in southern Ontario is a privilege to be enjoyed.

American Black Duck

Anas rubripes

THIS COMMON EASTERN DUCK lacks much of the colour of its marshland colleagues. Looking like a dark female Mallard, American Black Ducks are frequently overlooked because of their plain and dull appearance.

The identity of the American Black Duck is further complicated in midsummer, when other species molt into their eclipse plumage. Because feathers are lifeless (like our fingernails), they wear out and must be replaced. When ducks acquire their eclipse plumage, they forsake their courtship colours for dull tones. It is during this transformation that ducks are at their most vulnerable. When they are in the process of losing their flight feathers, many species are grounded for a few weeks until their feathers regrow. Ducks are inconspicuous at this stage, when they retire into peaceful wetlands to wait out the molt.

Quick ID: large duck; head and neck lighter than dark body; orange legs; purple speculum bordered by black; white wing linings in flight; **Male:** yellow bill; **Female:** dark green and black bill.

Size: 58 cm (22 in.)

Habitat: shallow lakes, ponds, agricultural fields, mud flats.

Nest: grass or sedge, lined with down; well concealed in vegetation or woodlands.

Food: grasses, non-woody plants, insects, seeds, aquatic invertebrates.

Foraging: grazes on land, tips up from the surface of wetlands.

Voice: soft, repetitive *quack quack quack.*

Similar Species: Mallard (hens and immatures, p. 33); Gadwall; other female dabbling ducks; eclipsed drakes.

Notes: Historically, the Mallard was the duck of the West and the Black Duck ruled the East. Recently, many Mallards have colonized eastern North America, largely at the expense of the Black Duck. These two ducks hybridize readily and produce viable offspring that closely resemble the Mallard parent. The hybrids retain characteristics from the Black Duck that enable them to withstand certain eastern parasites that can be fatal to pure Mallards.

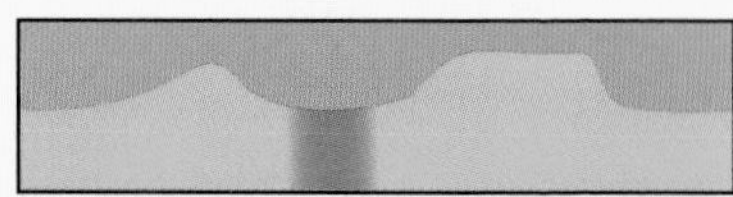

Mallard

Anas platyrhynchos

THE MALLARD IS THE CLASSIC DUCK—the male's chestnut breast and iridescent green head are symbolic of wetland habitat. These large ducks are commonly seen feeding in marshes, small lakes, farmers' fields and, during winter, along river edges and industrial cooling ponds. With their legs positioned under the middle part of their bodies, Mallards walk easily, and they can spring straight out of water without a running start.

Male Mallards pursue females energetically, but, like many other drakes, the male will abandon his mate soon after she's laid her eggs. This lack of parental commitment may seem harsh, but in fact it benefits the female and the ducklings. A colourful father could attract the attention of predators, placing the lives of the well-camouflaged female and ducklings at risk.

Quick ID: large duck; **Male:** iridescent green head; chestnut chest; white flanks; **Female:** mottled brown; with white border on purple speculum; bright orange bill and feet; sexes similar in late summer and fall, when male is in eclipse plumage.

Size: 58 cm (23 in.)

Habitat: widespread in city parks, agricultural areas, wetlands.

Nest: well-concealed grass nest, lined with down; usually close to water in dense vegetation.

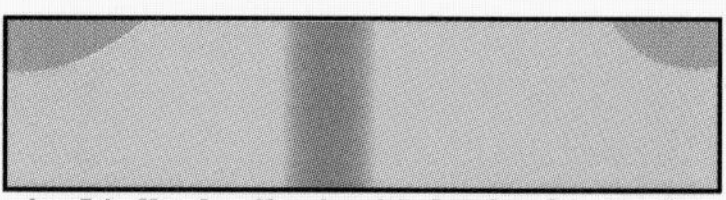

Food: vegetation, seeds, and waste grain.

Foraging: frequently feeds on land, also probes substrate of ponds by tipping up.

Voice: classic *quack-quack-quack.*

Similar Species: Northern Shovellers are white-breasted; female Mallards resemble American Black Ducks (p. 32) and many other female dabbling ducks.

Notes: Mallards are the most common duck in North America, and are easily seen year-round in southern Ontario. During the winter, rafts of Mallards mixed with other species are seen on open water. • Because Mallards molt several times a year, the heads of male Mallards are not always perfectly green.

Blue-winged Teal

Anas discors

THE MALE BLUE-WINGED TEAL has a thin, white crescent on its cheek and a steel-blue head to match its inner wing patches. These small ducks are extremely swift flyers, which frustrates their many predators. Their sleek design and rapid wingbeats enable teal to swerve even at great speeds, and also provide the small ducks the accuracy to make perfectly placed landings.

Unlike many of the larger dabblers, which migrate to the United States, teal overwinter in Central and South America. For this reason, Blue-winged Teal are often the last ducks to arrive in Ontario during the spring and the first to leave in autumn, usually by the end of September. On average, the smaller species of waterfowl migrate further, while the larger varieties don't undertake long migrations.

Quick ID: very small duck; **Male:** steel-blue head; white crescent on cheek; blue speculum; **Female:** small, plain; yellow legs; blue speculum.

Size: 39 cm (15 in.)

Habitat: marshes, small lakes.

Nest: well-concealed grass nest; in tall vegetation near water, lined with down.

Food: aquatic vegetation, seeds, aquatic invertebrates.

Foraging: graze on land, dabble.

Voice: Male: high-pitched *keck-keck-keck;* **Female:** faint *quack.*

Similar Species: female easily confused with other hens.

Notes: The Green-winged Teal and the Cinnamon Teal also occur in southern Ontario. The Green-winged, which is reasonably common, has a red face with a green swipe running back from the eye. The Cinnamon Teal, named for its overall colour, is a tough but rewarding find in south-central Ontario.

Common Goldeneye 

Bucephala clangula

THE COURTSHIP DISPLAY of this widespread duck is one of nature's most entertaining slapstick routines. The spry male goldeneye rapidly arches his large green head back until his bill points skyward, producing a seemingly painful *Kraaaagh*. Completely unaffected by his chiropractic wonder, he continuously performs this ritual to mainly disinterested hens. Feeding off the female's apathy, the male escalates his performance, creating a comedic spring scene that is appreciated more by birdwatchers than by the intended audience. When the female finally relents and pays attention to the quality of the various displays, the eager male, seemingly aware of his tenuous situation, reacts quickly, finalizing the pair's bond on the water's surface.

Quick ID: small duck; **Male:** large, dark green head; round, white cheek patch; white body; black back streaked with white; **Female:** chocolate-brown hood; sandy-coloured body.

Size: 47 cm (18 in.)

Habitat: northern woodland lakes, open water in winter.

Nest: tree cavities, abandoned woodpecker nests; usually near water.

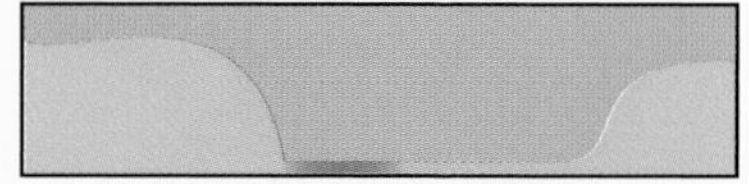

Food: aquatic invertebrates, aquatic vegetation, small fish.

Foraging: short dives.

Sound: wings whistle loudly in flight.

Similar Species: Hooded Merganser (p. 37) has a bold white crest; Bufflehead (p. 36) is smaller.

Notes: Because many large, dead trees have been removed from lakeside lots in Ontario, Common Goldeneye have lost many of their nesting sites. Goldeneye readily use nest boxes, so cottage owners can encourage these delightful birds to nest on their property.

Bufflehead

Bucephala albeola

HELD IN THE HIGHEST REGARD by naturalists, the small, fluffy Bufflehead is the 'cutest' duck in North America. A very reserved duck, the Bufflehead has simple plumage and a rotund physique. Found during summer on just about every inland lake, beaver pond, and wetland in the boreal forest, Buffleheads are rarely seen discrediting themselves by accepting handouts from humans.

Like their close relative the goldeneye, Buffleheads nest in cavities and have quite large heads. They were named for the shape of their head, which reminded an early ornithologist of a buffalo's. Regardless of head shape, the white slice behind the male's eye is diagnostic, because it does not have an outline. These feathered delights winter in southern Ontario, where they can be seen in the company of Common Goldeneye, in deep open water.

Quick ID: pigeon-sized; **Male:** tiny, round duck; white triangle on back of head; white body; dark back; **Female:** dirty brown; small white cheek patch.

Size: 34 cm (14 in.)

Habitat: breeds in Northern Ontario on woodland lakes and ponds, winters on Great Lakes and unfrozen waterbodies.

Nest: tree cavities lined with down.

Food: aquatic insects, water plants, small fish.

Foraging: short, shallow dives.

Voice: squeaky whistle, or hoarse croak.

Similar Species: Common Goldeneye (p. 35); Hooded Merganser (p. 37).

Notes: Preening is an important behaviour for birds because having feathers in good condition is vital for movement and for regulating temperature. In most birds (even chickens), the oil gland lies at the base of the tail and secretes a viscous liquid that inhibits bacterial growth and conditions feathers. After gently squeezing the gland with its bill, the bird methodically spreads the secretion over its feathers.

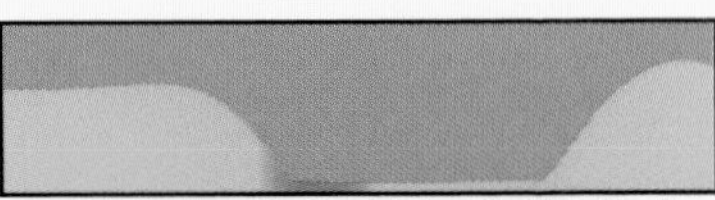

Hooded Merganser

Lophodytes cucullatus

LACKING DIVERSE FACIAL EXPRESSIONS, many non-human animals have evolved other means of sharing their feelings with others of their species. When aroused by danger or passion, a male Hooded Merganser flares his distinctive white crest. Unfortunately for the 'Hoodies,' many persistent birders are not satisfied until the crest is raised in alarm, producing a remarkable pose. The intrusion often causes the male to retreat, foregoing his everyday business at the expense of an overzealous birdwatcher. These mini-mergansers are delightful, and can be appreciated at a distance at many woodland lakes, or during the winter at cooling ponds and other areas of open water.

Quick ID: small duck; **Male:** large white patch outlined by black on head; white shoulder slash; dark back; brown body; **Female:** overall brown; shaggy; erectile crest.

Size: 46 cm (18 in.)

Habitat: woodland ponds, small lakes.

Nest: cavities lined with grass and down; usually near water.

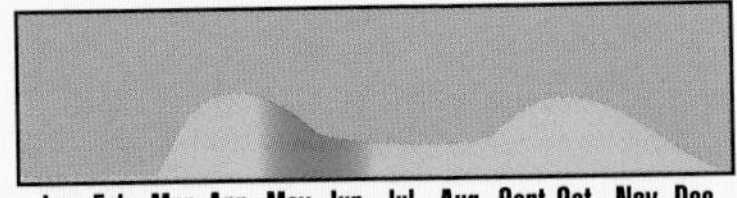

Food: small fish and aquatic invertebrates.

Foraging: long underwater dives.

Voice: frog-like *crooooo*.

Similar Species: Bufflehead (p. 36); Common Merganser (p. 38) lacks body colouration.

Notes: In Ontario, Hooded Mergansers are most frequently seen during the winter months. Because of the white patch on the male's head, large rafts of Common Goldeneye or Bufflehead should be double-checked to ensure that a Hooded Merganser was not initially overlooked.

Common Merganser

Mergus merganser

LOOKING LIKE A LARGE JUMBO JET taking off, the Common Merganser runs along the surface of the water, beating its heavy wings, until sufficient speed is reached for lift-off. Once in the air, our largest duck looks compressed and arrow-like as it flies strongly in low, straight lines.

Mergansers are lean and powerful waterfowl, designed for the underwater pursuit of fish. Unlike those of other fishers, a merganser's bill is saw-like, serrated to ensure that its squirmy, slimy prey does not escape. Common Mergansers are cavity nesters, breeding wherever there are suitable lakeside trees, and they are often seen on rivers. In Ontario, Common Mergansers are also seen during winter, when the large ducks congregate in rafts in areas of open water.

Quick ID: goose-sized; **Male:** well-defined dark green hood; white body; brilliant orange bill and feet; black spinal streak; **Female:** rusty hood; clean white throat; grey body.

Size: 64 cm (25 in.)

Habitat: large lakes and rivers, unfrozen water during winter.

Nest: often in tree cavities, sometimes on ground, occasionally in abandoned bird nests.

Food: small fish, amphibians, aquatic invertebrates.

Foraging: pursues fish by diving underwater.

Voice: Male: sharp croaks; **Female:** deep *karr.*

Similar Species: large ducks; Common Loon (p. 21); Red-breasted Merganser lacks white breast and orange bill.

Notes: This species is widespread and even is common in northern Europe. The British refer to the Common Merganser as 'Goosander.' • A similar bird, the Red-breasted Merganser, breeds throughout central and northern Ontario. Although the Red-breasted Merganser is less abundant than the Common Merganser, persistent naturalists will often encounter them on woodland lakes.

Turkey Vulture

Cathartes aura

THE TURKEY VULTURE'S seemingly effortless soaring is made possible by its great, silver-lined wings. Turkey Vultures seldom flap their wings, and they often rock from side to side as they scan forest clearings and shorelines. The way their wings angle upward in a shallow 'V' is a useful clue to their identity.

Turkey Vultures depend completely on carrion for food, and they have evolved a keen sense of smell. Their heads are featherless to keep them clean and parasite-free while they dig around inside carcasses. The Turkey Vulture's habit of regurgitating its rotting meal may be a defence mechanism that allows adults to reduce their weight for a quicker take-off, and gives the young vultures a powerful deterrent to would-be predators, who might prefer their food to smell a little fresher.

Quick ID: large hawk-sized; black, soaring bird; wings held in a dihedral position; silver-grey flight feathers; dark wing lining; small, red head; sexes similar.

Size: 69 cm (27 in.)

Habitat: open country, agricultural areas, Niagara Escarpment, possible everywhere except continuous forests.

Nest: none, eggs are laid on bare ground on cliffs, in caves, and among rocks.

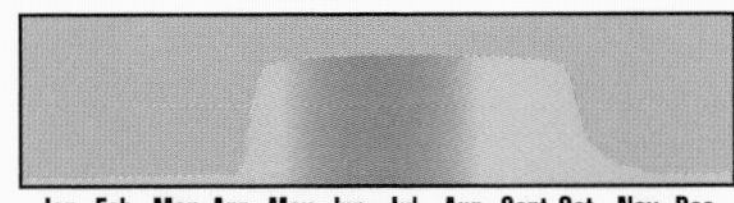

Food: carrion—all types, all sizes.

Foraging: high soaring.

Voice: not vocal.

Similar Species: large hawks and eagles have larger heads and generally hold wings flat in flight.

Notes: Turkey Vultures lack the crushing talons of most other raptors, because their food is already dead when they show up. Turkey Vultures rely on their sense of smell—more so than other birds—and have the ability to locate rotting carcasses buried under leaves and grasses.

Osprey

Pandion haliaetus

ON BENT WINGS, an Osprey surveys the calm water of a northern lake. Spotting a flash of silver at the water's surface, the Osprey folds in its great wings and dives toward the fish. An instant before striking the water, the large raptor thrusts its talons forward to grasp its slippery prey. The Osprey may completely disappear beneath the water to ensure a successful hunt, then it reappears, slapping its wings on the surface as it regains flight. Once it has regained the air, holding its prey facing forward, the Osprey shakes off the residual water and heads off toward its bulky stick nest.

A hungry Bald Eagle witnessing this remarkable hunting feat will not hesitate to pirate the meal. For many Osprey, a duel with a larger eagle is not worth the prized fish, so the fish is dropped and the Osprey returns to scan the steely surface of the lake.

Quick ID: large hawk; dark brown above; white below; dark 'elbow' patches; dark eyeline; flight profile is a shallow 'M'; sexes similar.

Size: 60 cm (23 in.)

Habitat: undisturbed northern lakes.

Nest: large, bulky stick structure; in trees, on utility poles, special platforms.

Food: almost exclusively fish.

Foraging: over water, dramatic dives.

Voice: sharp *kyew-kyew-kyew-kyew.*

Similar Species: Bald Eagles (p. 41) have a more distinctive head and tail; large hawks are usually not seen over large lakes.

Notes: Because fish are the Osprey's principle prey item, this bird has remarkable features to cope with their slimy and slippery skin. To prevent a squirmy escape, Osprey have specialized feet. Two of their toes face forward and two backward, and their soles are heavily scaled to enable them to clamp on tightly to slippery fish.

Bald Eagle

Haliaeetus leucocephalus

WHEN A BIRD is as large and charasmatic as the Bald Eagle, it is sure to receive attention from its human neighbours. Historically, Bald Eagles were relentlessly persecuted as varmints, and were shot as trophies. Recently, Bald Eagles have come to symbolize greatness, strength, and freedom. Although Bald Eagles may enjoy their current standing, neither extreme treats the bird without prejudice.

This secretive bird shuns the company of humans, preferring to retreat to large lakes where it can survey calm waters for ducks, fish, or an easier meal. Although the Bald Eagle has benefitted from recent human admiration, the only reward naturalists are likely to receive is a quick or distant glimpse of this attractive raptor—which usually is sufficient for an adrenaline surge that quickens the pulse.

Quick ID: large eagle; white head and tail (acquired at the age of 5); dark body; yellow bill and talons; imposing size; **Immatures:** lack white on head and tail but size and white streaks in wings are diagnostic.

Size: 90 cm (35 in.)

Habitat: large, undisturbed northern lakes, Great Lakes, cottage country.

Nest: huge stick nest, built upon yearly.

Food: carrion, fish, waterfowl.

Foraging: soars along shorelines looking for washed-up carcasses, occasionally plucks a fish or duck from the water's surface.

Voice: mechanical and unflattering *kleek-kik-ik-ik-ik*.

Similar Species: Osprey (p. 40) is much smaller and has black through the face; immatures may be confused with other large raptors.

Notes: Although the population of Bald Eagles is increasing in Ontario, sighting one of these magnificent raptors is always a memorable experience. Bald Eagles are best spotted during winter, near areas of open water. Industrial cooling ponds and outflows provide open water that attracts thousands of overwintering waterfowl. Such concentrations provide easy picking for Bald Eagles.

Northern Harrier

Circus cyaneus

THIS COMMON RAPTOR can best be identified by its behaviour. No other Ontario hawk is commonly seen flying low over fields and pastures during the day. The slow, lazy wingbeats of the Northern Harrier coincide with its undulating, erratic flight pattern. Unlike other hawks, which can find their prey only visually, the Northern Harrier stays close enough to the ground to listen for the birds, voles, and mice on which it feeds. When movement catches the Harrier's eyes or ears, it abandons its lazy ways to strike at prey with channelled energy.

Quick ID: hawk-sized; white rump; long tail and wings; low, coursing flight; facial disc seen only at close range; **Males:** grey; **Females and Young:** brown.

Size: 56 cm (21 in.)

Habitat: fields, wet meadows, and marshes.

Nest: flimsy nest of grasses, marsh vegetation and sticks; often on the ground in thick vegetation.

Food: small mammals, birds and nestlings, amphibians.

Foraging: low, methodical, coursing flights over open areas, swoops.

Voice: usually silent, rarely a weak *pee pee pee.*

Similar Species: Red-tailed Hawk (p. 45); Short-eared Owl has black elbow patches and deep wingbeats; other raptors lack white rump.

Notes: Just as Northern Harriers are making their last pass over hunting territories in the late evening, Short-eared Owls begin their nightly hunts. Both of these raptors prey on similar species, and hunt in much the same way. Because one hunts during the day, and the other at dawn and dusk, competition between the two is reduced—much to the dismay of their prey.

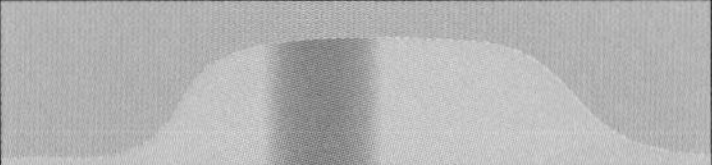

Sharp-shinned Hawk
Accipiter striatus

THIS SMALL FOREST HAWK is infrequently seen because it does not habitually soar, except during migration when it can be seen in great numbers. The Sharp-shinned Hawk is designed for quick, short flights, dodging tree trunks and branches in the pursuit of birds. When not chasing down its next meal, this hawk's flap-and-glide flight can be observed in mixed forests, as it either scouts over the tree tops or crosses small openings.

Its short, rounded wings, long, rudder-like tail, and long, piercing talons enable this raptor to prey almost exclusively on birds. Dramatic high-speed chases often end with the small hawk driving its razor-sharp talons through a coat of soft feathers, and then flying clumsily with its prey to a favourite feeding site. Sharp-shinned Hawks sometimes visit backyard feeders—not for the millet and sunflower seeds, but for the sparrows and finches the food attracts.

Quick ID: Blue Jay-sized; short, rounded wings; long tails are heavily banded; red horizontal streaking on breast; grey-blue back; **Immatures:** like adults but lack bold colour; **Females:** larger than males (like most birds of prey).

Size: 35 cm (13 in.)

Habitat: mixed woodlands.

Nest: mid-sized stick nest; in tall trees against the trunk or in a fork.

Food: almost exclusively songbirds, rarely small mammals, reptiles, amphibians, or invertebrates.

Foraging: high-speed chases of woodland birds dodging trees, catches prey in mid-air, prey frequently consumed at a traditional 'plucking post.'

Voice: unnerving and intense *kik-kik-kik-kik*.

Similar Species: Cooper's Hawk is larger, and the tip of its tail is more rounded; Merlin has pointed wings.

Notes: Accipiters (forest hawks) like the Sharp-shinned Hawk exhibit marked sexual dimorphism in size. Females are up to one and a half times the size of their mates, which may decrease competition between the pair over available food supplies.

Broad-winged Hawk
Buteo platypterus

THESE HAWKS are fairly secretive in their wooded breeding habitat, and frequently many summers can pass without one being seen. But, in migration, certain areas in Ontario can produce thousands in a single day! These inconsistencies in observation are not restricted solely to this species, but this may be the best example of a bird that both frustrates and rewards persistent birders.

Hawks' heavy wings are not designed for continual flapping flight, so these raptors seek out areas that reduce their need to flap. The Great Lakes and large bays in southern Ontario are quite daunting to Broad-winged Hawks, which prefer to skirt around the edges, funnelling through areas that provide welcome updrafts. Migrating raptors seek out rising thermals created by warm air, or air currents deflecting up from cliffs. The currents help them gain elevation before they launch across a stretch of stagnant heavy air.

Quick ID: crow-sized; barred, fan-like tail; horizontal russet streaks on chest; short, rounded wings; sexes similar.

Size: 41 cm (16 in.)

Habitat: dense deciduous or mixed-wood forests.

Nest: loose nest of sticks and twigs; high in a tree in dense forests.

Food: small mammals, birds, nestlings, insects.

Foraging: usually in forests, swoops from a perch.

Voice: high-pitched whistle, *peeeo-wee-ee.*

Similar Species: Red-tailed Hawk's (p. 45) tail is one colour; Sharp-shinned Hawk (p. 43) has a long, narrow tail; Rough-legged Hawk (p. 46) is a winter visitor; Red-shouldered Hawk has long wings and tail.

Notes: The updrafts that raptors use in migration are frequently referred to as 'kettles.' Today, some of the better-known kettles in Ontario can produce thousands of raptors during spring and fall migration, including many species of hawks, eagles, and falcons.

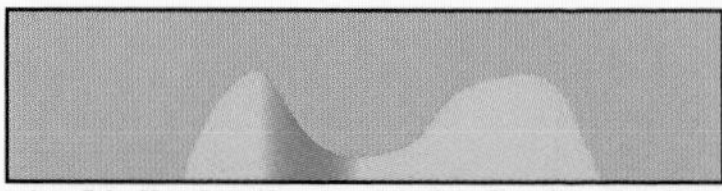

Red-tailed Hawk

Buteo jamaicensis

WITH ITS FIERCE facial expression and untidy feathers, the Red-tailed Hawk looks as though it has been suddenly and rudely awakened. Its characteristic scream further suggests that the Red-tailed Hawk is a bird best avoided. You would think other birds would treat this seemingly upset and rather large raptor with more respect, but the Red-tailed Hawk is constantly being harassed by crows, jays, and blackbirds.

The Red-tailed Hawk is well named, but it isn't until this hawk is two or three years old that its tail becomes brick red. The spotted 'belt' around its midsection and a dark leading edge to its wings are better field marks because they're seen in most Red-tails. Look and listen for these common hawks soaring above open country with nearby woodlands.

Quick ID: large hawk; adults have brick-red tail; most plumages have a thin brown belt; light flight feathers with dark wing lining; sexes similar.

Size: 56 cm (22 in.)

Habitat: open fields, pastures, and meadows with nearby woodlots.

Nest: bulky stick nest; in forks of tall trees, usually in woodlots.

Food: small rodents, snakes, large invertebrates.

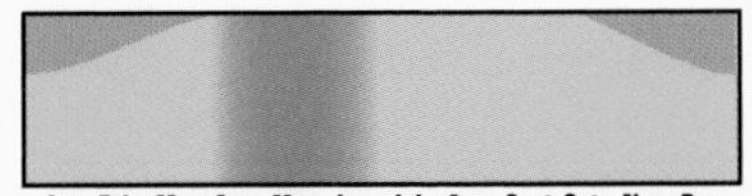

Foraging: swooping dives from tall perches or high soaring.

Voice: frequently heard loud, screaming *keeee-rrrr.*

Similar Species: Northern Harrier (p. 42) has a white rump; Broad-winged Hawk (p. 44) and Rough-legged Hawk (p. 46) both have banded tails.

Notes: One of the most widespread hawks in North America, the Red-tail occurs from the tundra to the Caribbean (its species name *jamaicensis* reinforces this broad distribution). Listen for its distinctive call, which is frequently heard in the background of many movies and TV shows.

Rough-legged Hawk
Buteo lagopus

FOR ATTENTIVE NATURALISTS, the first fall frost signals the return of the Rough-legged Hawk. These Arctic-nesting hawks appear to thrive in the misery of cold and snow, and vitalize empty winter landscapes with their hunting vigils. A country drive in the dead of winter would not be complete without spotting this great raptor, which often hovers over open fields. Mice and voles that leave their labyrinths of tunnels under the snow for a peek at the royal-blue winter sky are the Rough-legged Hawk's favourite prey item. The number of Rough-legs dining on Ontario rodents varies considerably from year to year. During mild winters the winter raptors can be quite common, but following a stretch of prolonged cold, even the hardiest of North American hawks chooses to continue south for gentler climates.

Quick ID: large, dark hawk; black belly; black elbow patch on wings; dark band on white tail; often hovers; much variation in plumage; sexes similar.

Size: 56 cm (22 in.)

Habitat: during winter, open fields and pastures.

Nest: of sticks and grasses; on rocky outcrops and cliffs in tundra areas, southern breeding limit is coastal Hudson Bay.

Food: small to mid-sized mammals, occasionally birds.

Foraging: soars over open ground, hovers, swoops.

Voice: occasional screech.

Similar Species: eagles; Red-tailed Hawk (p. 45); Northern Harrier (p. 42); Broad-winged Hawk (p. 44); all lack elbow patches and white base to the tail.

Notes: The species name of the Rough-legged Hawk, *lagopus*, means 'hairy foot' and refers to the bird's legs, which are feathered down to the toes—likely an adaptation to its cold habitat preferences. • Most hawks in Ontario are divided into two groups according to their genus: *Accipiter* and *Buteo*. Accipiters like the Sharp-shinned Hawk are forest dwellers, have long tails, and rarely soar, while Buteos have fan-shaped tails and are excellent soarers.

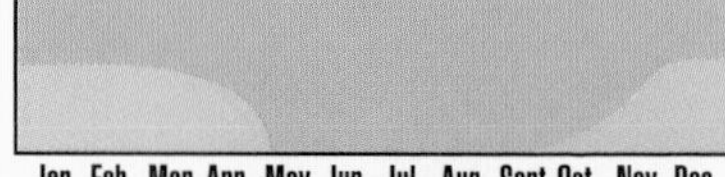

American Kestrel

Falco sparverius

THIS SMALL, NOISY FALCON is a common summer sight over much of Ontario. In areas where they do not overwinter, American Kestrels often appear in Ontario before the calendar or the weather announce the coming of spring. This bird has adapted well to rural life, and is commonly seen perched on power lines, watching for unwary grasshoppers, birds, and rodents. When not perched, American Kestrels can be seen hovering above potential prey. All falcons are skilled hunters; they have a unique, tooth-like projection on their hooked bills that can quickly crush the neck of small prey.

The nests of American Kestrels are often built in abandoned woodpecker cavities. Conservationists have recently discovered that kestrels will use nest boxes when natural cavities are unavailable, which should ensure that these active predators remain common throughout Ontario.

Quick ID: Blue Jay-sized; long, pointed wings; long tail; double black stripes on face; spotted breast; rapid wingbeat; hooked bill; **Male:** blue wings; russet back; colourful head; **Female:** russet back and wings.

Size: 27 cm (11 in.)

Habitat: open country, forest edges.

Nest: natural cavities, abandoned woodpecker holes, nest boxes.

Food: small birds, small mammals, reptiles, invertebrates.

Foraging: surveys open fields from an overhead perch or by hovering, then pounces.

Voice: fast, repetitive, shreaky *killy-killy-killy.*

Similar Species: Sharp-shinned Hawk (p. 43) has short, rounder wings; Merlin is larger, has a banded tail and lacks facial stripes.

Notes: The American Kestrel's species name *sparverius* is Latin for 'pertaining to sparrows,' an occasional prey item. Old field guides refer to this small falcon as the Sparrow Hawk. This name is no longer accepted—a good change since the American Kestrel is clearly neither a hawk nor a sparrow.

Killdeer

Charadrius vociferus

THE KILLDEER is one of the most widespread shorebirds in Ontario. It nests on gravelly shorelines, lawns, pastures, and occasionally on gravel roofs within cities. Its name is a paraphrase of its distinctive loud call and isn't an indication of its hunting habits.

The Killdeer's response to predators relies on deception and good acting skills. To divert a predator's attention away from a nest or a brood of young, an adult Killdeer (like many other birds) will flop around to feign an injury (usually a broken wing or leg). Once the Killdeer has the attention of the fox, crow, human, or gull, it leads the predator away from the vulnerable nest. After it reaches a safe distance, the adult Killdeer is suddenly 'healed' and flies off, leaving the predator without a meal.

Quick ID: larger than a robin; two black bands across breast; brown back; russet rump; long legs; white underbelly; sexes similar.

Size: 27 cm (11 in.)

Habitat: open areas, shorelines, fields, lawns, often far from water.

Nest: shallow scrape, little surrounding vegetation; often among gravel.

Food: terrestrial insects, aquatic invertebrates, seeds.

Foraging: gleans ground between running bursts.

Voice: loud, distinctive *kill-dee, kill-dee, killdeer-killdeer-killdeer* or variations thereof.

Similar Species: Black-bellied Plover has a black chest and occurs only as a migrant; Upland Sandpiper (p. 50) lacks black chest bands; Semipalmated Plover has a single chest band and migrates through southern Ontario.

Notes: A great many shorebirds filter through southern Ontario each year, and sorting through them is difficult for even the most experienced birdwatcher. An easy first step is to separate the plovers (like the Killdeer) from the sandpipers. Most plovers have shorter necks, are often striped, have three toes, and feed in a characteristic 'hit-and-run' technique. Most sandpipers are usually well camouflaged, have four toes and walk while feeding. As with any rule in nature's kingdom, there are of course exceptions, which are best learned through personal experience.

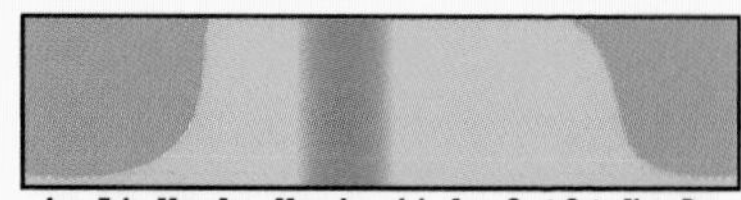

Spotted Sandpiper
Actitis macularia

THIS COMMON SHOREBIRD of our lakes and rivers has a most uncommon mating strategy. In a reversal of the gender roles of most birds, female Spotted Sandpipers compete for male mates in spring. After the nest is built and the eggs are laid, the female leaves to find another mate and the male incubates the eggs. This is repeated up to five times before the female settles down with one male to raise the chicks.

Spotted Sandpipers are readily identified by their arthritic, stiff-winged flight, low over the water. They're easily approached, and you can often get close enough to see their spotted breast.

Quick ID: smaller than a robin; **breeding:** spotted breast; olive-grey back; often teeters; yellow legs; yellow bill tipped with black; **Female:** spots more pronounced.

Size: 19 cm (8 in.)

Habitat: shores of lakes and rivers.

Nest: simple scrape, on ground, elevated among rocks, shrubs or tall vegetation; male incubates.

Food: invertebrates, including mollusks, flying insects.

Foraging: probes and gleans shorelines.

Voice: sharp, crisp *eat-wheat, eat-wheat, wheat-wheat-wheat-wheat.*

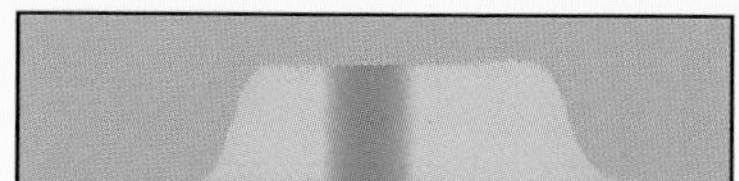

Similar Species: Dunlin (p. 51) is usually seen in large flocks; Lesser Yellowlegs has long, yellow legs; Killdeer (p. 48) has dark throat bands; many other migrant shorebirds.

Notes: Polyandry (mating strategy whereby one female mates with several males) is quite unusual in birds, because females invest so much energy in egg production. Like the Spotted Sandpiper, the three North American phalaropes (Red-necked, Red, and Wilson's) have females mating with several males. (All three migrate through southern Ontario, and the Wilson's breeds there.) These beautiful shorebirds are unlike Spotted Sandpipers; female phalaropes are much more colourful than their male counterparts.

Upland Sandpiper
Bartramia longicauda

IN LATE MAY the first Upland Sandpiper of the spring lands on a fencepost, and gracefully folds its long wings. The purposeful folding is not meant as a show, rather it's a tribute to the wings which have carried the shorebird a great distance. Having completed its 10,000 km (6200 mile) migration from the grasslands of South America, the bird relies on Ontario's bounty to raise a new generation of mighty migrants. For the next several months the male will keep a steady eye out for any predator, usually spying the landscape from a fencepost perch. As their chosen territory is generally treeless, their fencepost vantage allows the male to see and—fortunately for birdwatchers—to be seen. An approach by a curious naturalist will fail to close in on the ever-vigilant bird. Should a threat enter the male's realm he may cautiously dive at an intruder, but the dive will lack the enthusiasm he shows in his noble fencepost duty.

Quick ID: pigeon-sized; brown; small head; long neck; short bill; stiff-winged flight; often seen perched atop a fencepost or boulder; sexes similar.

Size: 31 cm (12 in.)

Habitat: open fields, grassy agricultural areas.

Nest: shallow depression lined with dry grass, vegetation often arches over nest.

Food: terrestrial invertebrates, often grasshoppers, seeds.

Foraging: plucks insects from ground and vegetation, gleans.

Voice: loud, 'haunting' whistle; call is a *kip-ip-ip-ip-ip*.

Similar Species: winter-plumage Black-bellied Plovers are often seen in small flocks, confusing only in late summer through early fall.

Notes: A bird such as the Upland Sandpiper is so perfectly linked to its habitat and behaviour that a name alone cannot do it justice. Until recently the Upland Sandpiper was called the Upland Plover—an honest mistake given that this bird does resemble a plover. • *Bartramia* is in honour of the ground-breaking and enthusiastic William Bartram, an early American botanist who discovered and described many species of eastern plants. His energy is certainly eternalized in the Upland Sandpiper.

Dunlin
Calidris alpina

THESE SMALL, PLUMP shorebirds are not in and of themselves remarkable. Outside of the breeding season, Dunlin are communal creatures, and it is the spectacular clouds of Dunlin that hold the magic of this species: individuals flying wingtip to wingtip, instantaneously changing course, tens of thousands behaving as one. These hypnotic flights, flashing alternating shades of white and black, are commonly seen as Dunlin migrate through southern Ontario, stopping over on shorelines and mud flats.

The unexplained communal flight of Dunlin leads many thoughtful observers to question accepted theories on social communication—profound questions drawn from the habits of a simple bird.

Quick ID: smaller than a robin; **breeding:** black; decurved bill; russet wings; black belly and legs; white line in wings; flocks often large; **non-breeding:** greyish-brown back; grey throat; white belly; sexes similar.

Size: 22 cm (9 in.)

Habitat: sandy or muddy shorelines, sewage lagoons.

Nest: on tundra; grass nest on a dry hummock.

Food: soft-bodied invertebrates, mollusks, insects, occasionally seeds.

Foraging: probes soft substrate, gleans shorelines.

Voice: quivering, like a bomb dropping.

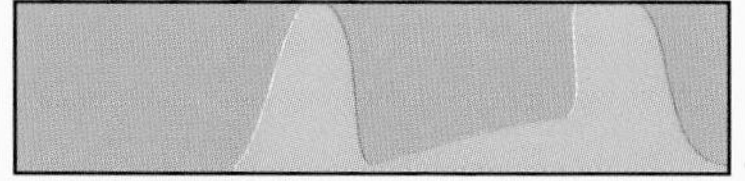

Similar Species: Semipalmated, Red, Pectoral, and Knot Sandpipers all have white bellies and straight bills.

Notes: The Dunlin is a species that also occurs in Europe and Asia. It was first given the name Dunling, but for reasons lost to science the 'g' was later dropped. • Large flocks of shorebirds were tempting targets for North American wild-game market hunters following the elimination of their principle prey, the Passenger Pigeon. When all but the last pigeons were shot out, the market hunters' rifles turned toward shorebirds, decimating many populations. Although the slaughter continued for just a few decades, Lesser Golden Plovers and Hudsonian Godwits remain uncommon to this day, and the Eskimo Curlew's existence is a speculative matter.

Common Snipe
Gallinago gallinago

ON WARM SPRING EVENINGS an eerie, rapid *who-who-who-who* can be heard over Ontario marshes. This common spring sound, with its hollow quality and increasing pace, comes from the vibration of the Common Snipe's stiff tail feathers as this abundant shorebird dives through its aerial display.

Although meetings with the Common Snipe are most often auditory encounters, this well-camouflaged bird occasionally reveals itself. Its long, straight bill, squat body and heavy streaking separate it from most other shorebirds. Although Common Snipes can be seen perched atop fenceposts near marshes, to fully experience this bird you must spend an evening at a marsh and listen as it carves a melody from the spring air.

Quick ID: larger than a robin; long, black-tipped bill; heavily streaked back; stocky, striped head; long legs; sexes similar.

Size: 27 cm (11 in.)

Habitat: marshes, moist meadows, bogs, swamps.

Nest: grass nest; well concealed in thick vegetation near water, on ground.

Food: soft-bodied invertebrates, insects, crustaceans.

Foraging: probes soft substrate, occasionally gleans vegetation.

Sound: delightfully eerie, accelerating *who-who-who-who-who-who.*

Similar Species: American Woodcock (p. 53) is plump, with shorter legs; other shorebirds are either too short of bill or not as heavily streaked.

Notes: The Common Snipe was formerly known as the Wilson's Snipe, in honour of Alexander Wilson, the father of American ornithology. • Ornithologists generate periodic lists of accepted common names for birds. The lists are useful because they eliminate confusion over regional preferences for common bird names, and because they reduce the need for people to know the often difficult scientific names.

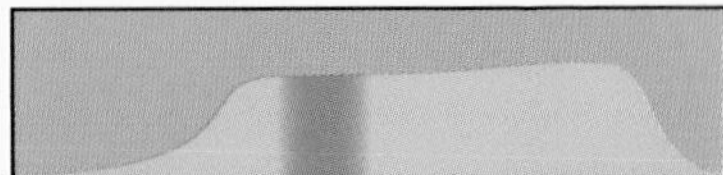

American Woodcock

Scolopax minor

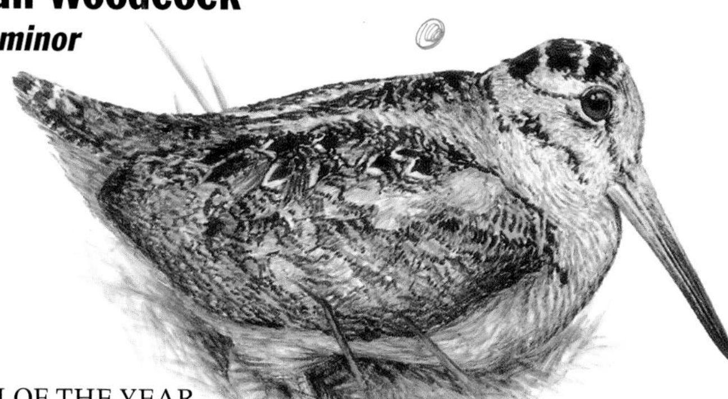

FOR MUCH OF THE YEAR, the American Woodcock's behaviour matches its cryptic and unassuming attire. Then, for a short month each spring, male woodcocks explode into vanity. The courtship performance begins when the male selects a small clearing in the woods, where his plaintive *bjeeent* inspires him to an Elvis-like boogie. Since the woodcock's legs are short, he usually selects a stage that is free of grass—thick vegetation would block the view hen woodcocks had of his swinging strut. When the male has sashayed sufficiently, he takes to the air to punctuate the show. Spiralling upward into the evening sky, he twitters increasingly toward the sky-dance climax. Upon hitting the peak of his ascent, the male woodcock relaxes, then plummets, uncontrolled, to the ground. Just prior to striking the ground, the woodcock pulls out of the crippled dive, and alights on his dancing stage, where he resumes his breeding ballet.

Quick ID: Blue Jay-sized; chunky; very short legs; very long bill; large eyes; rounded wings; barred crown; sexes similar.

Size: 28 cm (11 in.)

Habitat: moist woodlands.

Nest: on the ground; shallow depression lined with grass and leaves.

Food: mostly earthworms.

Foraging: probes deeply into soft substrate.

Voice: loud, nasal *bjeeent* (on ground), fluttering twitter and delicate warble in aerial courtship display.

Similar Species: Common Snipe (p. 52) has longer legs; other similar-sized shorebirds' bills are too short; Ruffed Grouse (p. 64) lacks long bill.

Notes: This bird is also known as the Bogsucker, Night Peck, and (my favourite) the Timberdoodle. • The large eyes of the woodcock are positioned so that the bird has an enveloping view (almost 360 degrees). The woodcock's long bill is a wonderfully dexterous tool. The dark tip is flexible, and the upper mandible can actually open.

Ring-billed Gull

Larus delawarensis

THIS WIDESPREAD GULL is also extremely common in southern Ontario. It is slightly smaller than the Herring Gull and has a distinctive dark bill ring. The Ring-billed Gull is a common sight in cities; it is frequently seen in parks or effortlessly soaring high overhead. The warm air rising from concrete and asphalt are like elevators that dozens of gulls ride simultaneously, climbing until their sleek shape vanishes into the sky.

Although these gulls appear to be regular urbanites, like so many Ontarians they commute daily into the cities. From shoreline suburbs, gull traffic can be seen during early mornings, congested along skyways leading into town. Their daily activities involve squabbling with other greedy gulls over leftovers from fast food-restaurants, and for food in open areas. When nicely fed, they may break from feeding duties by soaring high above the hectic pace of city life.

Quick ID: crow-sized; white head and body; light grey wings; black ring around end of bill; black wingtips; yellow legs; clear eyes; sexes similar.

Size: 45 cm (18 in.)

Habitat: urban, industrial, and agricultural areas.

Nest: communal nesters, in open or semi-open areas, shallow scrape on ground lined with grasses; often on low-lying islands or human-disturbed sites.

Food: fish, invertebrates, garbage, other birds' eggs.

Foraging: aerial patrols, gleans ground, surface dips.

Voice: high-pitched *hyjack-hyjack-hyjack*, also a low *yook-yook-yook.*

Similar Species: Herring Gull (p. 55) has pink feet; Black-backed Gull is relatively uncommon, has a dark back and wings and is seen primarily along the Great Lakes.

Notes: The Great Lakes attract many species of gull, many of them regulars while some are accidental. After spending time with Herring and Ring-billed Gulls, birdwatchers develop a good eye for unusual migrants. Glaucous and Iceland Gulls appear washed-out, because their wings are light-coloured. The Bonaparte's Gull and the Black-headed Gull each have a black head during the spring and dark 'ear' spots over winter. 'Gulling' can be very challenging, but most large concentrations usually contain something unexpected.

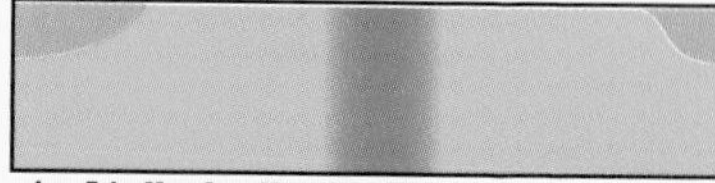

Herring Gull
Larus argentatus

MANY GULLS come and go in Ontario, but the Herring Gull is a year-round resident in the Great Lakes region. This 'sea gull,' familiar to all, does not rightfully deserve its moniker as the Herring Gulls seen in Ontario rarely venture to salt water. Many migrant gulls are more deserving of the name 'sea gull,' although if this bird were to relinquish the title, it would likely be labelled with one even less desirable. Large flocks of this gull can be found in bays, lakes, garbage dumps, shorelines, city parks, and agricultural fields. Herring Gulls are so widely distributed they are sure to be sighted on just about any birding trip taken along the shore of any large lake.

The Herring Gull is an engineering marvel. Agile on land, an effortless flyer, wonderfully adaptive, and with a stomach for anything digestible, Herring Gulls are perhaps the most widely distributed gull in North America.

Quick ID: larger than a hawk; white head and body; grey back; pink legs; dark wingtips; clear eyes; red spot on lower mandible seen only at close range; sexes similar; **Immatures:** variable, brown overall.

Size: 64 cm (25 in.)

Habitat: large lakes, garbage dumps, fields.

Nest: shallow scrape, under vegetation, often communal; usually on islands and peninsulas.

Food: opportunistic scavenger, eats young nestlings, garbage—almost anything.

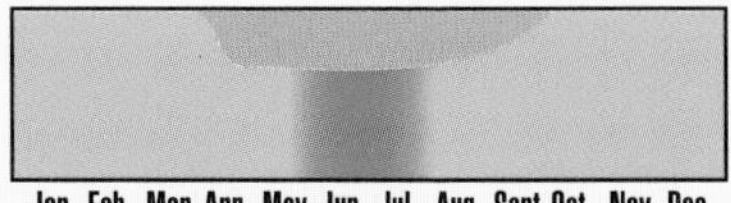

Foraging: pirates from other smaller birds, surface dips.

Voice: familiar scream: *hiyak-hiyak-hiyak*, also low *yuk-yuk-yuk*.

Similar Species: Ring-billed Gull (p. 54) has yellow legs and a banded bill; Great Black-backed Gull has a dark back and wings.

Notes: So why *don't* gulls' feet freeze when they spend entire days standing on ice? The feet and legs of birds are covered with scales, which prevents them from drying out. Additionally, the arteries and veins that bring the blood in and out of the birds' legs are in close contact, so much so that blood entering the leg is cooled by the blood leaving, while the blood leaving is warmed by the blood entering. This countercurrent exchange is quite effective for regular winter temperatures.

Common Tern

Sterna hirundo

THE COMMON TERN generally goes unnoticed until a splash draws attention to its headfirst dives into water. Once it has firmly seized a small fish in its black-tipped bill, the tern bounces back into the air and continues its leisurely flight.

Although terns and gulls share many of the same physical characteristics, there are features that clearly separate the two groups. Terns seldom rest on the water, and they rarely soar in flight. They also have very short necks, pointed wings and long, forked tails, and they tend to look toward the ground during flight. These characteristics should help identify the Common Tern.

Quick ID: larger than a pigeon; black cap; orange bill tipped with black; grey back and wings; pointed wings; white throat and belly; forked tail; often hovers; sexes similar.

Size: 37 cm (15 in.)

Habitat: large lakes and bays.

Nest: shallow scrape, little nest material; on beaches, shorelines, and other sparsely vegetated areas.

Food: small fish, aquatic invertebrates.

Foraging: aerial dives.

Voice: *kee-arr*, often calls from the air.

Similar Species: Forster's Tern has a grey tail and frosted wingtips; Arctic Tern is a migrant with an all-red bill; Caspian Tern is gull-sized.

Notes: The Common Tern will not hesitate to use artificial nesting structures. Bridge pilings and breakwalls are commonly used by this tern. • The species name *hirundo* means 'swallow-like' and refers to flight and physical similarities. • The Common Tern is widely distributed in the Northern Hemisphere.

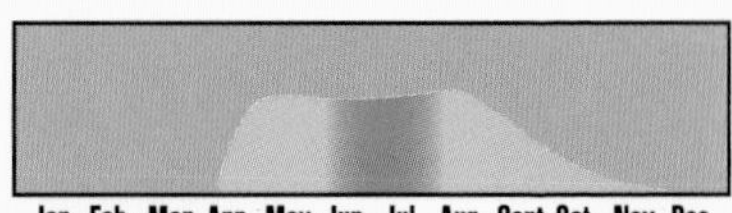

Black Tern
Chlidonias niger

IN MID-FLIGHT, this black aerial acrobat has the agility to catch elusive dragonflies and to snatch aquatic insects from the water's surface. Like large swallows, Black Terns dip and spin in mid-air as though to defy the laws of flight that restrict most other birds. These incredible manoeuvres can be observed over the marshes, sloughs, and small lakes where these terns feed. Although dainty overall, Black Terns may be the most pleasant birds to watch fly, as their routine dips and spins make them one of the most aerobatic species in Ontario.

In order to spell this tern's scientific name correctly, one must misspell *chelidonias*, the Greek word for 'swallow.' When the Black Tern was first described and named, the author accidentally left out the 'e,' a mistake that now must be repeated for the name to be correct.

Quick ID: robin-sized; black head and belly; grey back and wings; pointed wings; forked tail; white undertail coverts; sexes similar.

Size: 25 cm (10 in.)

Habitat: freshwater marshes, small lakes.

Nest: raised, of wet vegetation; always in dense emergent vegetation.

Food: flying insects, small fish, aquatic invertebrates.

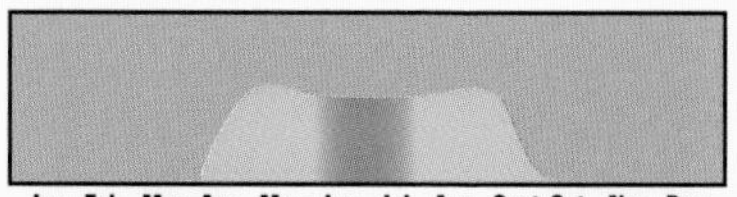

Foraging: hawks for flying insects, skims water surface.

Voice: metallic *krick-krick*.

Similar Species: dark swallows are much smaller; Common Tern (p. 56) is grey and white.

Notes: Although it may be a useful memory aid, terns were not named for the undeniable agility they have performing turns in the air. Tern is simply a derivation of the Old Norse word for tern, *therna*. • The Black Tern is a very widespread species, breeding in North America, Europe, Africa, Asia, but not Australia—yet.

Eastern Screech Owl
Otus asio

DESPITE ITS small size, the Eastern Screech Owl is a mighty hunter, with a varied diet ranging from insects it catches in mid-air to grouse that outweigh this small owl. Silent and reclusive by day, Screech Owls leave their daytime roosts to hunt at night.

Owls' senses are refined for darkness and silence. Their forward-facing eyes have many times more light-gathering sensors than ours do, and their wings are edged with frayed feathers for silent flight. Their ears, located on the sides of their heads, are asymmetrical (one is higher than the other), giving these birds stereophonic hearing that enables them to track sounds more easily. Given all these adaptations, it is to no one's surprise that owls have successfully invaded nearly all of the world's ecosystems.

Quick ID: smaller than a robin; with ear tufts; heavy vertical streaking on chest; two colour phases, red and grey; sexes similar.

Size: 22 cm (9 in.)

Habitat: mature deciduous forests, orchards, city parks.

Nest: natural tree cavities, large woodpecker holes, occasionally in nest boxes.

Food: small rodents, shrews, birds, invertebrates.

Foraging: swoops from a perch, occasionally flycatches.

Voice: haunting, descending whinny or whistle, horse-like.

Similar Species: Great Horned Owl (p. 59) is twice as large and has horizontal breast streaking; Northern Saw-whet Owl (p. 62) has a dark facial disc and no ear tufts.

Notes: The call of the Eastern Screech Owl is well known to Ontarians who spend early spring evenings in forested areas. • The scientific names of this and another Ontario owl, the Long-eared Owl, contain the same two words: *asio* and *otus*. *Otus* is Greek for 'ear,' while *asio* is Latin for 'horned owl.' Despite the similarity in names, the Eastern Screech Owl (*Otus asio*), and the Long-eared Owl (*Asio otus)* are not each other's closest relative.

Jan Feb Mar Apr May Jun Jul Aug Sept Oct Nov Dec

Great Horned Owl
Bubo virginianus

THIS COMMON NOCTURNAL hunter is among the most formidable of predators. Great Horned Owls use both their specialized hearing and their human-sized eyes to hunt mice, rabbits, grouse, amphibians, and rarely, fish. They have a poorly developed sense of smell, which may be why these owls are the only consistent predator of skunks. Worn-out and discarded Great Horned Owl feathers are therefore often identifiable by a simple sniff.

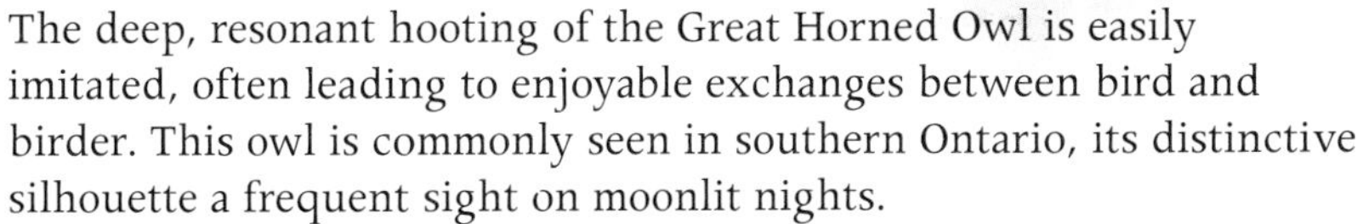

The deep, resonant hooting of the Great Horned Owl is easily imitated, often leading to enjoyable exchanges between bird and birder. This owl is commonly seen in southern Ontario, its distinctive silhouette a frequent sight on moonlit nights.

Quick ID: hawk-sized; with ear tufts; fine, horizontal chest streaking; plumage from light grey to dark brown; sexes similar.

Size: 56 cm (22 in.)

Habitat: widespread in woodlots and mature forests, often seen along open areas.

Nest: abandoned nests of Red-tailed Hawks or other raptors, occasionally in natural tree cavities.

Food: small mammals, rabbits, skunks, grouse, amphibians, rarely fish.

Foraging: swoops from a perch.

Voice: slow, low hoots, *eat my food, I'll-eat you.*

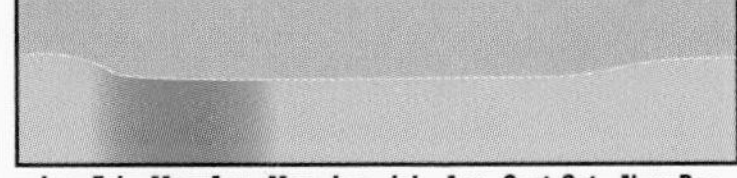

Similar Species: Barred (p. 60), Great Gray, and Snowy Owls (p. 61) all lack ear tufts; Eastern Screech Owl (p. 58) is much smaller, with vertical breast streaking; Long-eared Owl's ear tufts are closer together, and it has a slimmer body with vertical barring on chest.

Notes: All owls (and many other raptors) regurgitate pellets. These pellets are the indigestible parts of their prey, compressed into an elongated ball. The feathers, fur, and bones that make up the pellets are interesting to analyze, since they reveal which species the owl has recently eaten. Although these pellets may appear disgusting, they are generally quite clean and dry. Look for owl pellets under frequently used perches.

Barred Owl

Strix varia

TUCKED AGAINST A GREAT TRUNK or perched on a broken limb, the Barred Owl begins its nightly hunt. The soft brown eyes and deadly accurate ears scan the darkening forest for motion. A rustle, a twitch—a vole scurries a distance away. Excited, the owl orients itself to the noise by systematically jerking its head—up, down, and side to side—cueing itself to the rodent's sound. On silent wings, the Barred Owl launches itself and floats down to the darkened forest floor. Crashing through grasses and shrubs, the owl seizes the vole, crushing it with strong, sharp talons. After swallowing the rodent whole, the owl flies lazily back up to its perch, patiently awaiting the next vole to unknowingly challenge the owl's hunting instincts.

Quick ID: smaller than a hawk; dark eyes; horizontal streaking around throat; vertical streaking on chest; sexes similar.

Size: 53 cm (21 in.)

Habitat: mature mixed-wood or coniferous forests, often near lakes or rivers.

Nest: natural tree cavities, abandoned nests.

Food: small rodents, squirrels, shrews, amphibians.

Foraging: swoops from a perch, occasionally pounces from flight.

Voice: distinctive *who cooks for you, who cooks for you all?*

Similar Species: This is the only Ontario deep-forest owl with dark eyes.

Notes: Spring nights in the north woods echo with the amazing call of the Barred Owl. The hooting calls between a pair often escalate into a hooting frenzy. Their calls are easily imitated, and the thrill of joining in the madhouse chorus is most memorable. But take care—your voice will be perceived as a threat, and might provoke a spirited attack from the easily stressed and territorial owls.

Snowy Owl

Nyctea scandiaca

WHEN ALL OTHER ANIMALS have either migrated far to the south or are comfortably snuggled in their winter dens, the Snowy Owl confronts winter blizzards by perching defiantly atop the highest viewpoint. Even in the worst winter weather, this ghostly visitor is shielded from the cold by a thick feathery coat that almost hides its black bill and talons.

Snowy Owls become whiter with age, gradually losing the dark spots of their youth. Their presence in southern Ontario during winter depends on the availability of prey in their Arctic breeding grounds. If northern lemmings and voles are scarce, many Snowy Owls head south for the winter, where dozens of them may be seen daily in agricultural areas or on off-shore islands.

Quick ID: hawk-sized; white; black bill and talons; yellow eyes; wings rounded in flight; **Mature Males:** almost all-white; **Females:** larger size, dark spots; **Juvenile Males:** have dark spotting on white body.

Size: 58 cm (23 in.)

Habitat: in winter, open fields and agricultural areas.

Nest: tundra, on raised hummock; lined with lichens or grass.

Food: in winter, voles and mice, occasionally birds.

Foraging: swoops from a perch, often punching through snow layer.

Voice: non-vocal.

Similar Species: Great Horned Owl (p. 59) is darker, with ear tufts; Great Gray Owl is grey overall and is usually uncommon in southern Ontario.

Notes: Feathers are one of nature's best insulators. As birds ruffle their feathers, they create air pockets between their own body temperature and the ambient temperature. The more pockets, the better the insulation. • The Snowy Owl may be white for a variety of reasons. As a species frequently found in snowy surroundings, its colour may offer some concealment. White coats may also act as greenhouses for white polar animals, as the transparent (white) plumage or fur let heat waves in, but does not release them.

Northern Saw-whet Owl

Aegolius acadicus

CRASHING THROUGH the dense understorey of a mature forest, a naturalist ducks to pass under a thicket. When he pops up on the other side, he meets a small owl face to face. The Northern Saw-whet Owl is a cute pixie, tame by the standard of most Ontario birds, and inquisitive. Perched an arm's length away, the owl bobs its rounded head, its unblinking eyes studying the surprised intruder. The urge to touch the animated bird is overwhelming; its calm behaviour apparently begs for contact. Barely larger than the outstretched approaching hand, the Saw-whet maintains its pleasant, undisturbed expression. Minutes pass with eyes locked in stare, as if both creatures were searching for answers held by the other. The hand stops short of breaking the human-wildlife barrier, and the human retreats toward fellow naturalists.

Quick ID: smaller than a robin; rounded head; reddish streaks on white breast; dark bill; dark facial disc; sexes similar.

Size: 20 cm (8 in.)

Habitat: mature mixed-wood or coniferous forests.

Nest: natural cavities, woodpecker holes.

Food: mice, voles, shrews, invertebrates.

Foraging: swoops from a perch.

Voice: soft whistles, slightly faster than one per second.

Similar Species: The Boreal Owl has a light bill and vertical 'eyebrows'; the Eastern Screech Owl (p. 58) has ear tufts.

Notes: Northern Saw-whet Owls are much more frequently heard than seen. Their easily imitated whistle, offered into late winter woods, often yields a response. • The Boreal Owl of northern Ontario is very similar in sound and appearance. The Boreal is so uncommonly seen that it is one of the birds most sought after by North American birders.

Horned Lark
Eremophila alpestris

THE HORNED LARK is probably most frequently observed as it rises in front of a speeding vehicle on gravel roads in open country. Its way of cutting off to the side or overtop of the vehicle just prior to a fatal collision shows the agility of the Horned Lark. This small songbird's first instinct is to run rather than fly, however, and the speeds it can attain on foot are quite remarkable. Although the Horned Lark's habit of running is distinctive, as are its 'face mask' and 'sideburn' markings, the black tail that contrasts with the rest of its body is unique among open-country songbirds, and it is unmistakable as the bird flies out of harm's way.

Horned Larks are found in every type of unforested area—tundra, clearcuts in northern forests, mountain tops, sea coasts, and open fields and grasslands. In areas of Ontario where Horned Larks don't overwinter, they are among the first songbirds to arrive in late March.

Quick ID: larger than a sparrow; overall brown with black bib and mask; black headband leads to small 'horns' (often not seen); black tail; light belly; sexes similar but female slightly duller.

Size: 18 cm (7 in.)

Habitat: open country, pastures, ditches, fields.

Nest: on ground; shallow depression lined with fine materials.

Food: insects, seeds.

Foraging: gleans ground and vegetation.

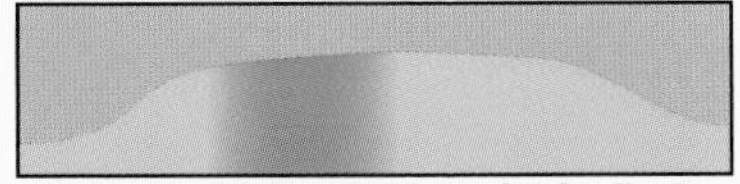

Jan Feb Mar Apr May Jun Jul Aug Sept Oct Nov Dec

Voice: high-pitched tinkling, often sung from the air.

Similar Species: sparrows lack facial stripes and black tails.

Notes: The Horned Lark is a bird of the open country, and it is a remarkable runner. Many Horned Larks that breed in the tundra and in Ontario congregate during winter. The flocks, which occasionally number over 100,000 birds, can be seen tumbling low over fields in the latter parts of winter.

• The much-celebrated lark in literature and song is not the Horned Lark (although its voice is pleasant), but a European relative.

Ruffed Grouse

Bonasa umbellus

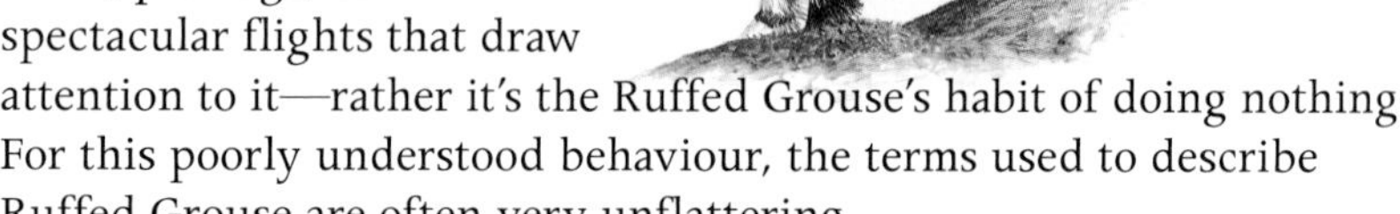

HIKERS ARE OFTEN amazed at the Ruffed Grouse. It is not this bird's voice, plumage, or spectacular flights that draw attention to it—rather it's the Ruffed Grouse's habit of doing nothing. For this poorly understood behaviour, the terms used to describe Ruffed Grouse are often very unflattering.

It is not out of stupidity that grouse freeze, remaining motionless despite the advances of curious onlookers. In reality, this adaptation serves this and other grouse well, because their plumage provides the birds with effective camouflage. It's probable that for every grouse that is encountered, many more are overlooked, thanks to their defence behaviour. It is likely, therefore, that in the majority of grouse-human interactions, it is the birds who marvel smugly at the dull-sensed passersby.

Quick ID: chicken-like; mottled brown or reddish-brown (two colour phases); multi-banded tail; black shoulder patch not always evident; crest raised only in alarm and arousal; sexes similar.

Size: 43 cm (17 in.)

Habitat: continuous and broken deciduous and mixed-wood forests.

Nest: well-concealed, shallow depression lined with leaves or grass; on the ground, beside log or tree.

Food: buds, flowers, seeds, occasionally insects.

Foraging: browses, gleans, usually on the ground, occasionally in the trees.

Sound: courtship drumming produced by wings, deep, hollow booms delivered at an accelerated pace (like a lawnmower starting up).

Similar Species: American Woodcock (p. 53) has a long bill; Ring-necked Pheasant has a much longer tail and splendid colours; Gray Partridge has a chestnut belly; Spruce Grouse is darker overall and has a black throat and belly.

Notes: During winter, the toes of Ruffed Grouse grow scaly bristles along the outer edge. These act as snowshoes for the grouse, which often wades through snow to feed. Another adaptation for winter weather is the Ruffed Grouse's habit of spending cold nights burrowed into snow banks. • The sound of the Ruffed Grouse is a pleasant and mysterious sound in spring woods. The sound is often incorrectly thought to come from the wings striking the bird's chest, but all the wings beat is the air.

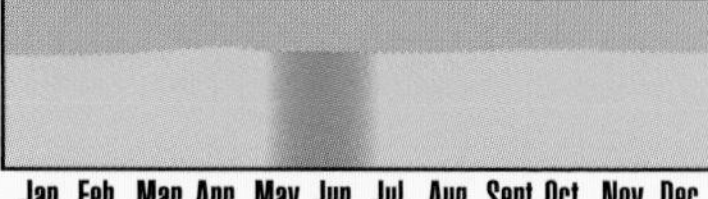

Rock Dove
Columba livia

THE ROCK DOVE (or Pigeon) is very dependent on human society for food and shelter. This Eurasian native lives in old buildings, on ledges and bridges, and it feeds primarily on waste grain and human handouts. Although these common city birds appear strained when walking—their heads moving back and forth with every step—few birds are as agile in flight.

Rock Doves are perfectly woven into rural and urban life in Ontario, and they are abundant in city parks. While no other bird varies as much in colouration, white, red, blue, or mixed-pigment Pigeons all have a flashy white rump. To withstand the coldest temperatures, these year-round residents simply ruffle their feathers and crouch in a corner out of the wind.

Quick ID: pigeon; colour variable, from iridescent blue-grey, red, white; usually has white rump; orange feet; fleshy base to the bill; sexes similar.

Size: 32 cm (13 in.)

Habitat: cities, towns, farms.

Nest: on ledges of buildings, bridges or natural cliff faces; mud saucer mixed with plant matter.

Food: waste grain, seeds, plant matter.

Jan Feb Mar Apr May Jun Jul Aug Sept Oct Nov Dec

Foraging: gleans ground, picks off seeds.

Voice: soft, rolling *coorrr-coorrr.*

Similar Species: Merlin (in flight), does not hold its wings in a 'V' when gliding.

Notes: All members of the pigeon family (including doves), feed 'milk' to their young. Since birds lack mammary glands, this isn't true milk but a product produced by glands in the bird's crop. The chicks insert their bills down the adult's throat to eat the thick liquid. • The renowned Dodo Bird, now extinct, was a large and flightless pigeon.

Mourning Dove

Zenaida macroura

THE PEACEFUL CALL of the Mourning Dove diffuses quickly through forest stands and echoes the lonely spirit of the countryside. This plaintive, comforting sound is sometimes mistaken for a baby's mumble by Ontarians unfamiliar with the vocalization of this common bird. Tracing the low, soothing call to its source can be frustrating as the hollow quality to the notes and the bird's motionlessness often do not betray its secretive perch.

This native member of the pigeon family is widespread throughout southern Ontario. Mourning Doves are swift flyers, and when they explode into flight their wingtips clap above and below their bodies. In flight these sleek, long-tailed doves fly with grace, and they're always accompanied by a faint whistling of wind through their wings.

Quick ID: pigeon-sized; olive-brown plumage; long, white-trimmed, tapering tail; slim, sleek body; shiny dark patch below ear; sexes similar.

Size: 31 cm (12 in.)

Habitat: woodlots, agricultural areas, broken forests.

Nest: loose twig nest, lined with fine plant materials; in trees.

Food: seeds, waste grain.

Foraging: gleans ground and vegetation, picks off seeds.

Voice: *cooo-cooo-coooah.*

Similar Species: Black-billed Cuckoo (p. 104) has a white breast and no white on tail; Yellow-billed Cuckoo has a dark back with white underparts.

Notes: The Mourning Dove is one of the most widespread species in North America, and it is still expanding its range. With the extinction of the Passenger Pigeon about 100 years ago, there is a large niche to be filled in the biotic community of the East. The expansion of agriculture has also been to the advantage of the Mourning Dove, which regularly feeds on waste grain.

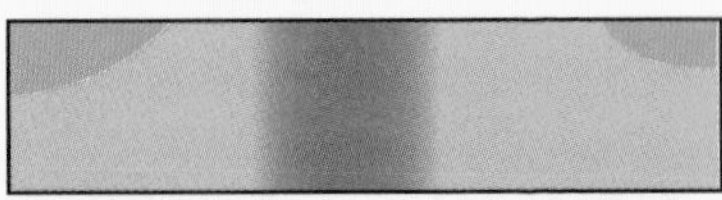

Common Nighthawk
Chordeiles minor

THE COMMON NIGHTHAWK has two distinct personalities—mild-mannered by day, it rests on the ground or on a horizontal tree branch, its colour and shape blending perfectly into the texture of the bark. At dusk, the Common Nighthawk takes on a new form as a dazzling and erratic flyer, catching insects in flight.

To many people, the call of the nighthawk is a sound of summer evenings, and the recent declines in their numbers have left many naturalists longing for the previously common calls. The fascinating courtship of Common Nighthawks occurs over forest openings, beaches, and urban areas. The nighthawks repeatedly call out with a loud, nasal *peeent* as they circle high overhead, then they dive suddenly toward the ground and create a hollow 'vroom' sound by thrusting their wings forward at the last possible moment, pulling out of the dive.

Quick ID: robin-sized; cryptic light to dark brown; pale throat; white wrist bands; long, pointed wings; tail has shallow fork in flight; flight is erratic; sexes similar.

Size: 24 cm (10 in.)

Habitat: widespread; open forests, agricultural areas, cities.

Nest: none, lays eggs on bare ground in well-drained areas, on sandy soil, gravel rooftops.

Food: flying insects.

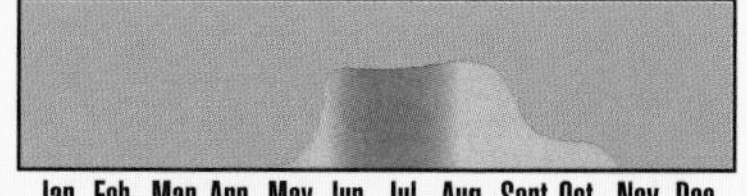

Jan Feb Mar Apr May Jun Jul Aug Sept Oct Nov Dec

Foraging: catches insects on the wing.

Voice: nasal *peeent*.

Similar Species: Whip-poor-will (p. 68) and Chuck-will's-widow have rounded wings and tail.

Notes: The Common Nighthawk and the Whip-poor-will belong to the same family as the nightjars, frogmouths, and goatsuckers (all are unrelated to true hawks). These colourful names reflect the bizarre behaviour and morphology of these birds. • Spring nights are also filled with the very similar *bjeeent* call of the American Woodcock. The nighthawk's call originates from the air, while the woodcock calls from the ground.

Whip-poor-will
Caprimulgus vociferus

THE WHIP-POOR-WILL makes identification easy for novice birdwatchers because this nighttime hunter fills the late evening with its own name. The distinctive *whip-poor-will* call is repeated continually from dusk to dawn, with the bird stopping only to swallow a mouthful of moths. Because Whip-poor-wills and nighthawks feed entirely on flying insects, these birds have remarkable adaptations for this tricky foraging technique. Although it may not appear evident on resting birds, these birds have a very wide gape, great big eyes, and their mouths are surrounded by vibrissae (naked feather shafts that funnel insects into the open mouth).

Quick ID: robin-sized; grey-brown plumage; wings and tail rounded and outer tail feather light when spread; sexes similar.

Size: 25 cm (10 in.)

Habitat: open forests with clearings.

Nest: none, lays eggs on bare ground in woodland clearings.

Food: flying invertebrates, especially moths.

Foraging: catches flying insects on the wing.

Voice: clear *whip-poor-will*, repeated often, at close range phrase terminates with a hiccup.

Similar Species: Common Nighthawk (p. 67) has pointed wings, forked tail, and white wrist bands; Chuck-will's-widow inhabits extreme southern Ontario and is slightly larger and lighter in colour.

Notes: There are other birds in this family named for their calls, notably the Chuck-will's Widow and the Common Poorwill (which naturally doesn't include the word 'common' in its call). • The Common Poorwill, found to the south and west of Ontario, is the only bird known to enter a hibernation-like sleep. During cold nights, this bird enters a state of prolonged sleep known as 'torpor,' in which its metabolism slows significantly. The Whip-poor-will avoids cold conditions by migrating to South America.

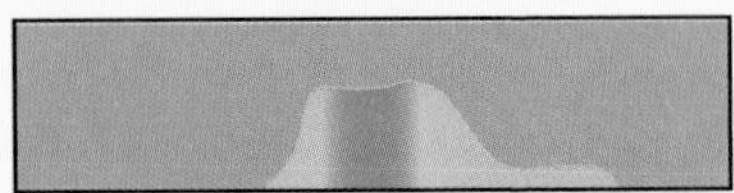

Chimney Swift

Chaetura pelagica

FILLING THE SKIES above forest clearings and wetlands with its gentle, twinkling voice, the Chimney Swift spends most of its waking hours on the wing in vigilant search of flying insects.

Swifts are shaped much like swallows—long, tapering wings, small bills, wide gape, and long, sleek body—but they share no close phylogenetic relationship. The wingbeat of swifts looks uncomfortable, but it doesn't hamper the graceful flight of these aerial masters, which cast a boomerang silhouette when they glide. Swifts, when not in flight, use their small but strong claws to cling precariously to vertical surfaces. Because many old, hollow hardwood trees have been removed since colonization, Chimney Swifts have adopted human structures as common nesting sites.

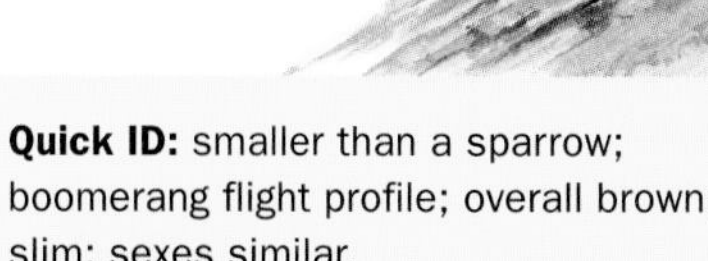

Quick ID: smaller than a sparrow; boomerang flight profile; overall brown; slim; sexes similar.

Size: 13 cm (5 in.)

Habitat: cities, open forests, agricultural areas.

Nest: attached to wall, chimney or hollow tree; saucer-shaped, of twigs bound together with saliva.

Food: flying invertebrates.

Foraging: catches insects on the wing.

Voice: distinctive chatter.

Similar Species: All swallows have smooth, direct flight.

Notes: As the name suggests, a common nest site of these swifts is within chimneys. • The Chimney Swift is one of the frequent flyers of the bird world; only sleeping and incubation keep swifts off the wing. It has been suggested that during the brief four- or five-year lifespan of the Chimney Swift, the small bird flies several million kilometres.

Ruby-throated Hummingbird

Archilochus colubris

YOU ARE FORTUNATE if you are one the few to get a prolonged look at a Ruby-throated Hummingbird, the only eastern hummingbird. Most meetings are over before they begin—a loud hum draws your attention to a small object flitting about, but it quickly disappears through the trees. It's often only after the bird has disappeared that its identity becomes apparent.

Fortunately, Ruby-throated Hummingbirds are easily attracted to feeders of sweetened water. The male's iridescent ruby throat and emerald back play with the sunlight in ever-switching colours. The Ruby-throated Hummingbird's gentle appearance is misleading; these fiercely aggressive hummingbirds will chase intruders away in spirited defence of a food source.

Quick ID: our smallest bird; iridescent green back and wings; long, dark bill; **Male:** has ruby throat.

Size: 10 cm (4 in.)

Habitat: mixed woodlands, cities, manicured gardens.

Nest: on tree limb; tiny cup made with spider silk and plant matter.

Food: nectar, small invertebrates, sap.

Foraging: hovers while probing flowers and hummingbird feeders with bill.

Voice: weak chatters and squeaks (most often heard during fights).

Similar Species: no other hummingbirds breed in Ontario.

Notes: Since hummingbirds occur only in the New World (North and South America), early explorers and naturalists were fascinated by these tiny wonders. • Hummingbirds do not hitch-hike on geese or other large birds in migration (as once thought), they fly to Central America on their own. Ruby-throated Hummingbirds are among the most rapid of fliers; they can cross the Gulf of Mexico in migration more quickly than most other birds.

Belted Kingfisher

Ceryle alcyon

THIS MEDIUM-SIZED BIRD is always associated with water. As its name suggests, kingfishers prey primarily on fish, which they catch with precise headfirst dives. A dead branch extending over calm water will often serve as a suitable perch for the Belted Kingfisher to survey the fish below.

These year-round residents are found near open water, but are never far from shore. They build their nests at the ends of burrows, often dug a few feet deep into a sandy bank. A rattling call, blue-grey colouration, and large crest are the distinctive features of the Belted Kingfisher. With most birds, the males are more colourful, but female Kingfishers are distinguished from males by the presence of a second, rust-coloured belt.

Quick ID: pigeon-sized; blue-grey back, wings, head and chest band; shaggy crest; heavy bill; **Female:** has a rust-coloured belt.

Size: 33 cm (13 in.)

Habitat: lakes, slow-moving streams and rivers, wetlands.

Nest: earth burrow in a stream bank, often more than 1 m (3 ft.) deep.

Food: fish, aquatic invertebrates, amphibians.

Foraging: dives into water from a perch or from an overhead hover.

Voice: fast rattle.

Similar Species: none.

Notes: Although there are many species of kingfisher in the world, there is only one in Ontario (and barely three in North America). • All kingfisher feet are syndactyl—two of the three forward-facing toes are fused. They dig their long burrows with their bills and their claws.

Red-headed Woodpecker

Melanerpes erythrocephalus

"His tri-coloured plumage, so striking… A gay and frolicsome disposition, diving and vociferating around the high dead limbs of some large tree, amusing the passenger with their gambols."

—Alexander Wilson

WHEN WILSON LANDED in North America, the Scotsman with little money and few skills did not know what he'd do in the New World. Like a revelation, a Red-headed Woodpecker was one of the first birds to greet the immigrant. Never had Wilson seen such beauty, and the bird inspired the future father of American ornithology to devote his life to birds. With no formal ornithological background, he went on to discover and describe dozens of North American species. Although the Red-headed Woodpecker's plumage may not drive everyone to great scientific achievements, its beauty impassions all who see it.

Quick ID: robin-sized; stunning red head and throat; black wings and tail; white rump, inner wing patches and belly; sexes similar.

Size: 24 cm (10 in.)

Habitat: deciduous forests, river edges, city parks.

Nest: cavities, usually in snag or dead limb; lined with wood chips.

Food: insects, seeds, nuts.

Foraging: hammers into infested tree trunks and limbs, flycatches.

Voice: loud squawk: *Ker-r-r-ruck* or loud *queer queer queer.*

Similar Species: Red-bellied Sapsucker; other woodpeckers; no other Ontario woodpecker has an all-red head.

Notes: The scientific name of the Red-headed Woodpecker is as straightforward as its English name. *Melanerpes erythrocephalus* simply means 'the black creeper with a red head.'• This beautiful woodpecker can be attracted to backyard feeders by suet, sunflower seeds, and corn.

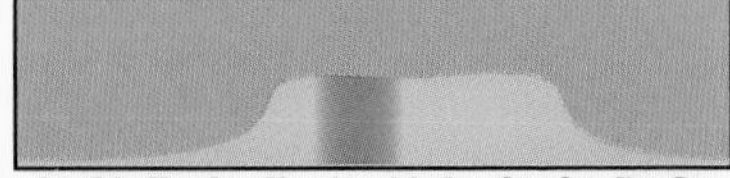

Yellow-bellied Sapsucker

Sphyrapicus varius

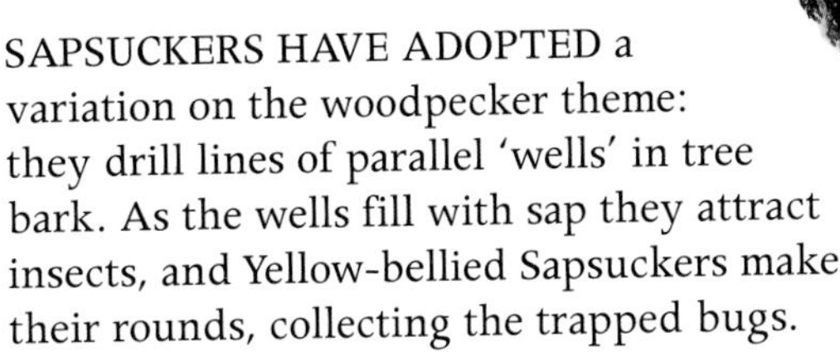

SAPSUCKERS HAVE ADOPTED a variation on the woodpecker theme: they drill lines of parallel 'wells' in tree bark. As the wells fill with sap they attract insects, and Yellow-bellied Sapsuckers make their rounds, collecting the trapped bugs.

Some people find the damaging effect on trees overshadows the bird's resourcefulness, but most healthy trees can withstand a series of sapsucker wells. Hummingbirds certainly enjoy the sapsucker's ability to plan in advance—so much so that they will flit by to pilfer the trapped insects and sap while the sapsucker is away. Without sapsucker wells, some hummingbirds would die in freak spring snowstorms that blanket flowering plants.

Yellow-bellied Sapsuckers are among the easiest woodpeckers to identify by ear. They often meow like a cat, and their territorial drumming sounds are random, like Morse code.

Quick ID: smaller than a robin; black and white back and wings; black bib; yellow wash on belly; red forehead; **Male:** has a red throat.

Size: 22 cm (9 in.)

Habitat: mature mixed-wood and coniferous forests.

Nest: cavities, usually in a deciduous tree with heart rot, preferably birch or aspen.

Food: insects, fruit, sap, berries.

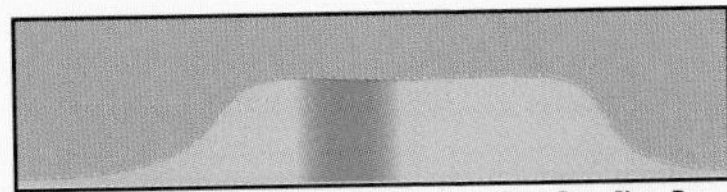

Foraging: picks insects caught in wells, flycatches.

Sound: call is cat-like *meoow*, drumming sounds like Morse code.

Similar Species: other woodpeckers lack black bib and red forehead.

Notes: The sapsucker's genus name *Sphyrapicus* is derived from the Greek *sphura* ('hammer'), and the Latin *picus* ('woodpecker'). • Glaciation and geographic barriers have resulted in several closely related species of sapsucker, including the Red-naped and the Red-breasted, both of which are found well to the West.

Downy Woodpecker

Picoides pubescens

SOFT TAPS CARRY THROUGH a quiet forest, sounding out the activities of a Downy Woodpecker. It searches for hidden invertebrates methodically, by chipping off dead bark and probing into crevices. The woodpecker's small bill is amazingly effective at removing tiny slabs of bark, which rain down to the forest floor. Only when all the nooks of a tree have been probed will the Downy look about, and give a chipper note before moving on to explore neighbouring trees.

This black and white bird is the smallest North American woodpecker and is common in wooded ravines and city parks. It's easily attracted to backyard feeders by suet. The male is readily distinguished from the female by a small patch of red feathers on the back of its head.

Quick ID: larger than a sparrow; black and white wings and back; white underneath; short, stubby bill; white outer tail feather spotted black; **Male:** has red patch on back of head.

Size: 17 cm (7 in.)

Habitat: mature mixed-wood and deciduous forests, city parks.

Nest: tree cavities, needing an opening only the size of a golf ball.

Food: insects, seeds and nuts.

Foraging: hammers infested tree trunks and limbs.

Voice: '*pik*' note; whinny call.

Similar Species: The Hairy Woodpecker (p. 75) is larger, with a longer bill and clean white outer tail feathers.

Notes: Woodpeckers are able to go about vertically because of their feet and their tails. The feet of woodpeckers are zygodactyl, meaning two toes face forward and two backward (the exceptions are the three-toed woodpeckers). These clamping feet, coupled with a stiff tail that woodpeckers prop against trunks, enable these birds to go vertical.

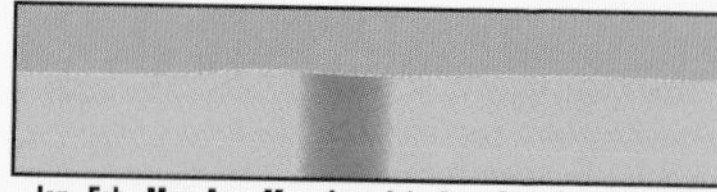

Jan Feb Mar Apr May Jun Jul Aug Sept Oct Nov Dec

Hairy Woodpecker
Picoides villosus

THE HAIRY WOODPECKER looks like an overgrown Downy Woodpecker, and shares the habitat of its smaller cousin. Although not as common or as easily approached as the Downy, the Hairy's loud calls and hammering enliven an empty winter forest. Its long, dark bill hammers rotting wood apart, exposing the soft-bodied larval invertebrates inside. Many woodpeckers are dependent on dead and dying trees for nest sites and stable food sources. The perception that dead wood and old trees are waste is a view not shared by many species of woodpecker. By hammering apart old logs and feeding on invertebrates, woodpeckers contribute to the renewal process inherent in natural systems.

Quick ID: robin-sized; black and white back and wings; white underneath; bill as long as head is wide; no black spots on white outer tail feathers; **Male:** has red patch on back of head.

Size: 24 cm (10 in.)

Habitat: mature mixed-wood and coniferous forests.

Nest: cavity the size of a tennis ball; lined with wood chips.

Food: insects (adult and larval), seeds and nuts.

Foraging: hammers infested tree trunks and limbs.

Voice: sharp '*pik*' note; whinny.

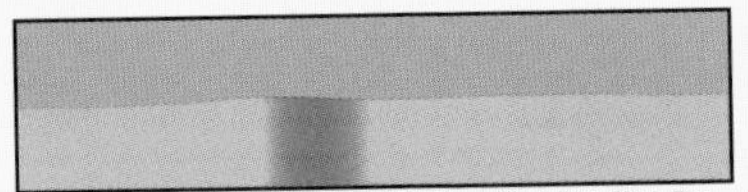

Similar Species: The Downy Woodpecker (p. 74) is smaller, with a shorter bill; the Black-backed Woodpecker has a solid black back.

Notes: Hidden within a woodpecker's bill is the secret to its wood-boring ways. The tongues of most woodpeckers are very long, in some cases more than four times the length of the bill. The long-reaching tongue of woodpeckers is made possible by twin structures that wrap around the perimeter of the skull. The tip of a woodpecker's tongue is sticky and finely barbed to seize even the most stubborn wood-boring insects. The nostrils of the Hairy Woodpecker (and other woodpeckers) are covered in feathers, which filter out the sawdust created by hammering.

Northern Flicker
Colaptes auratus

THE NORTHERN FLICKER is a woodpecker, but its behaviour is often more similar to a robin's. Flickers are the most terrestrial of the North American woodpeckers; they're often seen on the ground, feeding on ants or taking a dust bath. Often it is only when the Northern Flicker is around its nest cavity that it truly behaves like other woodpeckers—clinging, rattling, and drumming.

The Northern Flicker has spotty plumage, a black bib, and in flight, its white rump is distinctive. Old field guides refer to the Northern Flicker as the Yellow-shafted Flicker, the name having been changed fairly recently. Northern Flickers are easily seen throughout the spring and summer, and occasionally a few overwintering birds visit backyard feeders when snow blankets the ground.

Quick ID: pigeon-sized; brown barred back; spotted underneath; black bib; white rump; yellow wing and tail linings; long bill; grey crown; **Male:** has a black mustache.

Size: 32 cm (13 in.)

Habitat: deciduous, mixed-wood, or coniferous forests, agricultural areas.

Nest: cavities; usually in snag, occasionally in nest boxes.

Food: ants, other insects, seeds.

Foraging: picks ants from the ground, hammers infested tree trunks and limbs.

Voice: two-syllable squawk: *kik-kik kik-kik....*

Similar Species: The Red-bellied Woodpecker has a red crown and no spots on its breast.

Notes: To rid themselves of parasites, birds often resort to a behaviour called 'anting.' Unusual as it sounds, Northern Flickers (among others) squish ants and then preen themselves with the remains. Ants contain concentrations of formic acid ('ant' in French is *fourmie*), which kills small parasites living off the flickers' skin and feathers.

Pileated Woodpecker

Dryocopus pileatus

THE LAUGHING CALL and rhythmic drumming of the Pileated Woodpecker echo through the stands of mature forests. With its powerful bill and stubborn determination, our largest woodpecker chisels out rectangular cavities in its unending search for grubs and ants. The distinctive cavities are often the only evidence that a Pileated Woodpecker is in a forest. These crow-sized woodpeckers are secretive and retiring birds, and seeing them is always an unexpected surprise. Watching the swooping flight and flashing white underwings, or catching a glimpse of this red-crested bird clinging to a hollow snag, are precious moments that birdwatchers seek out.

Quick ID: crow-sized; mostly black; white wing linings; flaming red crest; **Male:** has a red mustache and a red crest that extends through the forehead.

Size: 42 cm (17 in.)

Habitat: mature, continuous coniferous and deciduous forests.

Nest: cavities, fist-sized holes, often rectangular; lined with wood chips.

Food: insects, especially ants, some fruit, nuts.

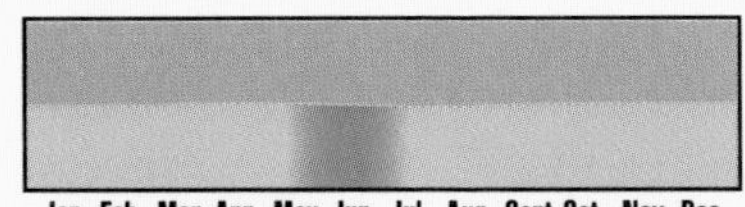

Foraging: drills infested tree trunks and limbs, often near base of tree.

Voice: laughing *kik-kik-kik-kik*.

Similar Species: American Crow (p. 90) and Common Raven (p. 91) have no white in their wings; other woodpeckers are much smaller.

Notes: Although many cleared areas of Ontario are beginning to revert back to forest, a pair of Pileated Woodpeckers requires about 50 hectares (100 acres) of mature forest to settle. • A common argument among birders is whether this species' common name is pronounced 'pie-lee-ated' or 'pill-e-ated'—take your pick and move on to more interesting things.

Olive-sided Flycatcher

Contopus borealis

A LARGE BEE WEAVES through the crowns of a black spruce bog, surveying the moist forest floor for flowering plants. The swift insect attracts the attention of an Olive-sided Flycatcher perched atop a stunted tree. The bird launches after its prize and, after a few quick flaps of its wings, seizes the bee in mid-air. Holding its catch firmly in its bill, the bird loops back and lands on the same perch it vacated moments earlier. This is the art of flycatching, and the Olive-sided Flycatcher is a master of this thrilling feeding technique.

No errant bee is safe flying into the range of the Olive-sided Flycatcher, and no northern bog is free of this bird's distinctive call. Offered from the highest spruce, the Olive-sided Flycatcher's *quick three beers* is very distinctive.

Quick ID: smaller than a robin; dark olive vest with tufts of white 'shirt hanging out'; white throat and belly; dark tail and flight feathers; olive head and back; sexes similar.

Size: 19 cm (8 in.)

Habitat: coniferous forests, often in bogs and wet areas.

Nest: cup-shaped nest on horizontal conifer branch; of grass and fine materials.

Food: flying insects.

Foraging: flycatches.

Voice: lively *quick three beers.*

Similar Species: other flycatchers; Eastern Phoebe (p. 81); Eastern Wood-Pewee (p. 79); all lack dark vest.

Notes: Although flycatching is a perfectly reasonable term to describe the activities of most flycatchers, there are other terms used to describe the same foraging method. 'Hawking' or 'sallying' for insects mean the same as flycatching; the terms are used interchangeably, despite the confusion caused to novice birdwatchers.

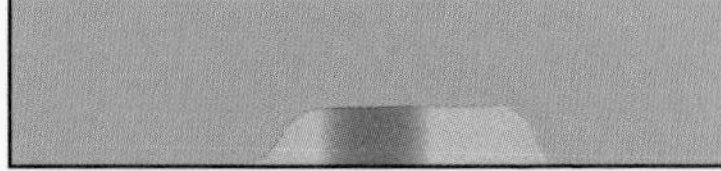

Eastern Wood-Pewee
Contopus virens

THE EASTERN WOOD-PEWEE'S clear, descending call rings continuously throughout the early summer months. At the tops of tall shade trees, this flycatcher sings its simple but distinct song, as if in defiance of the heat and humidity.

Like all other flycatchers in Ontario, the Eastern Wood-Pewee relies primarily upon insects for food. The quick, short, looping bursts known as 'flycatching' can be pleasant to watch, and it's interesting to note the bird's catching statistics. Enthusiastic naturalists can follow the flight of caddisflies, damsel flies, and other slow-flying insects as they unknowingly fly into the bird's range. By spending time watching which insects are taken and which are avoided, you can observe the food preferences of predators and the defence mechanisms of prey animals.

Quick ID: sparrow-sized; overall olive-grey, darker on wings and tail, lighter on throat and belly; upper mandible dark, lower mandible light; no eye-ring; two wing bars; sexes similar.

Size: 16 cm (6 in.)

Habitat: deciduous forests, urban parks, in areas free of dense understorey.

Food: flying insects, invertebrates, occasionally berries.

Foraging: flycatches, occasionally gleans vegetation.

Nest: cup-shaped, made with grasses and soft materials; built on horizontal branch, usually high in trees.

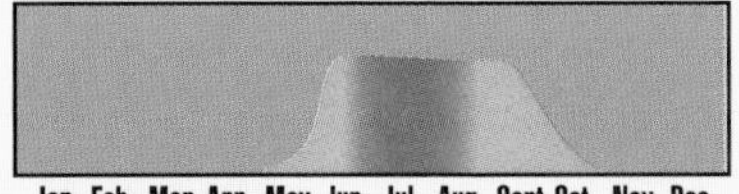

Voice: song: often repeated, flat *pee-o-wee;* call: descending *peee-errr.*

Similar Species: Alder (p. 80) and Least Flycatchers have an eye-ring; Eastern Phoebe (p. 81) lacks wing bars.

Notes: Because insects have been preyed upon for so long, they are the masters of defence. Many flying insects eat plants that make them distasteful or even poisonous to their predators, and they flaunt their foul flavour with vivid colours. Because of the distinct colours, it is unlikely that a bird will try eating another one after having experienced the unpleasant taste. Ever the opportunists, many perfectly tasty insects have adapted to appear very much like their poisonous allies, a strategy which protects a few of the flavourful critters from birds like the Eastern Wood-Pewee.

Alder Flycatcher

Empidonax alnorum

THE ALDER FLYCATCHER belongs to a select group of birds that both thrills and challenges birdwatchers of all levels. The empidonax flycatchers (named after their genus) occur throughout North America, and are famous in birdwatching circles for being notoriously hard to identify. Their plumages have slight variations that are obvious only under ideal conditions, and they all behave in much the same manner. The only hopes that birdwatchers have in telling these birds from each other are habitat and voice.

Southern Ontario is an exceptionally rich area for flycatchers; the Alder, Least, and Willow Flycatchers are frequently seen, and the Acadian and Yellow-bellied Flycatchers make rare appearances. All of their calls are distinctive and simple, so 'birding by ear' is necessary in empidonax cases. The Alder sings a hearty *free-beer*, the Least sings *Que-bec*, and the Willow sings a chipper *fitz-bew*. Despite the identification problem posed by these flycatchers, their antics are worth experiencing no matter what their names are.

Quick ID: sparrow-sized; olive green overall; white eye-ring; two wing bars; dark bill; yellow wash on belly; dark wings and tail; sexes similar.

Size: 15 cm (5 in.)

Habitat: moist alder or willow thickets bordering rivers or lakes.

Nest: cup-shaped nest of grasses and soft materials; built into a forking branch.

Food: flying insects, other invertebrates, occasionally berries, seeds.

Foraging: flycatches, occasionally gleans vegetation.

Voice: crisp, quick *free beer.*

Similar Species: Least, Willow, and Acadian Flycatchers; Eastern Wood-Pewee (p. 79); Eastern Phoebe (p. 81); all best identified by sound.

Notes: *Empidonax* is a wonderful name for these endearing birds—it means 'lord of the mosquitoes.' • The Alder Flycatcher is usually found in thickets that border a stream or wetland, while the Willow Flycatcher prefers open areas with a shrub layer. The Least Flycatcher is perhaps the most widespread of the three in Southern Ontario, and its call is frequently heard in semi-open deciduous forests.

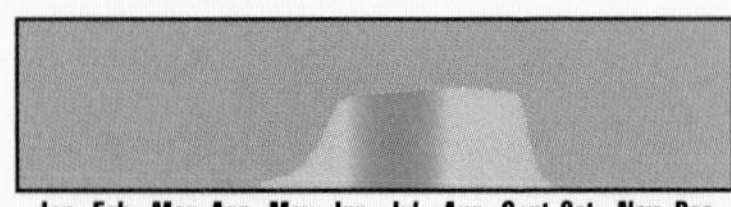

Eastern Phoebe

Sayornis phoebe

ALTHOUGH MANY BIRDS pump their tails while perched, no bird can match the zest and frequency of the Eastern Phoebe's tail wag. This early spring migrant may lack distinctive plumage, but its identity is never questioned when the quick and jerky tail rises and falls. Keeping in perfect synchrony with its rhythmic rump, the Eastern Phoebe's voice joins in accompaniment. As its name suggests, this small flycatcher bolts out a cheery *fee-bee,* from an exposed spring perch. The Eastern Phoebe is one of the first songbirds to return in the spring, and since it frequently builds its nest on buildings, its courtship and nest-building behaviours are easily observed. The nest site may be used repeatedly over the years, or a new site may be chosen annually. Whatever the case, the Eastern Phoebe's nest is always protected from the rain by a roof.

Quick ID: larger than a sparrow; brownish-grey back; no wing bars or eye-ring; dark tail, wings and head; yellowish belly; sexes similar.

Size: 18 cm (8 in.)

Habitat: agricultural areas, open woodlands.

Nest: cup-shaped mud nest; built under ledges on barns, in picnic shelters, abandoned buildings, culverts, on bridges.

Food: flying insects, invertebrates, berries, seeds.

Foraging: flycatches, occasionally gleans vegetation.

Voice: bold and often repeated *fee-bee fee-brreee.*

Similar Species: all other flycatchers have wing bars or distinctive field marks.

Notes: Ornithologist Charles Lucien Bonaparte (nephew of Emperor Napoleon) chose to honour Thomas Say by naming the genus of the three North American phoebes (*Sayornis*) after that great entomologist. Unfortunately, this gracious act has led to some confusion. While only the Eastern Phoebe actually says *fee-bee*, a western bird is called the Say's Phoebe even though it sings *pee-ter*.

Great-crested Flycatcher

Myiarchus tyrannylus

THE GREAT-CRESTED Flycatcher is most unusual in its selection of decor for its nest cavity: it occasionally lays a shed snakeskin as a door mat. This uncommon but noteworthy practice can identify the nest of this flycatcher, the only member of its family in Ontario to nest in a cavity. The objective of the Great-crested Flycatcher's infrequently seen nest decoration is not known, and these versatile birds have occasionally substituted plastic wrap for reptilian skin.

The Great-crested Flycatcher's name is somewhat misleading as this bird's crest can only truthfully be considered 'great' when compared to those of other flycatchers. If the crest of this tyrant flycatcher were measured against that of the Blue Jay, Cardinal, or Waxwing (birds with names not reflecting their crested crowns), it would certainly have to forfeit its 'Great-crested' title.

Quick ID: smaller than a robin; yellow belly; grey throat and head; dark back and wings; chestnut tail lining; erectile crest; sexes similar.

Size: 20 cm (8 in.)

Habitat: open forests, small woodlots, prefers those adjacent to edges.

Similar Species: other flycatchers; Eastern Wood-Pewee (p. 79); Eastern Phoebe (p. 81); all are smaller and lack lemon-yellow belly and chestnut tail lining.

Food: flying insects, invertebrates, some berries, seeds.

Foraging: flycatches, occasionally gleans vegetation.

Nest: old woodpecker cavities, occasionally in nest boxes; bulky nest seen through hole, infrequently with a shed snakeskin hanging from the opening.

Voice: robin-like *whee-eep.*

Notes: Although there are roughly 26 different groups of living birds in the world (known scientifically as 'Orders'), about 60 per cent of all bird species belong to one order, the Passerines or perching birds. This ratio holds true for southern Ontario's breeding birds as well, as the perching birds (flycatchers, swallows, corvids, warblers, sparrows, finches, etc.) outnumber all other orders combined. In this book, the Passerines begin at the Olive-sided Flycatcher and end with the House Sparrow.

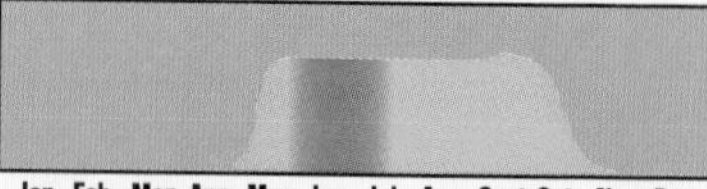

Eastern Kingbird
Tyrannus tyrannus

WHEN ONE THINKS of a tyrant, images of a large carnivorous dinosaur or a menacing ruler are much more likely to come to mind than the image of a little bird. While the Eastern Kingbird may not initially seem to be as imposing as other known tyrants, this flycatcher certainly lives up to its scientific name, *Tyrannus tyrannus*. The Eastern Kingbird is pugnacious—it will fearlessly attack crows, hawks, other large birds and even humans that pass through its territory. The intruders are often vigorously pursued, pecked, and plucked for some distance, until the kingbird is satisfied that there is no further threat.

The courtship flight of the Eastern Kingbird, which can be seen in fields and shrubby areas, is characterized by short, quivering wingbeats, a touching display even for this little tyrant.

Quick ID: smaller than a robin; black head, back, wings and tail; white underneath; white terminal tail band; orange crown (rarely seen); sexes similar.

Size: 22 cm (9 in.)

Habitat: agricultural areas, hedgerows, shrubby areas.

Nest: on horizontal branch; cup-shaped nest made of grass and fine materials.

Food: flying insects, other invertebrates, berries.

Foraging: flycatches, occasionally gleans vegetation.

Voice: sharp, single *dzeet* or frequently repeated *kitter-kitter*.

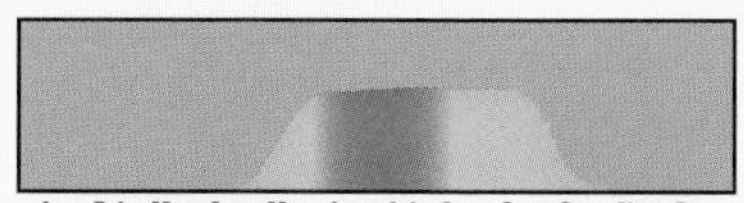

Similar Species: all other flycatchers; Tree Swallow (p. 85); all lack white terminal tail band and are not black and white.

Notes: Birds harassing other birds is a frequently observed behaviour, and is usually in defence of a nest site. Predatory birds are the ones most frequently pursued, but there is a hierarchy to the chases. Chickadees are known to harass Saw-whet Owls, while Gray Jays will annoy all other owls. Crows are the favourite targets of kingbirds and blackbirds, but crows in turn frequently harass hawks. Harassing is a curious behaviour to observe, as it is undoubtedly the smaller bird who is the aggressor and driving away the other, which is often twice as large.

Purple Martin

Progne subis

LATE SUMMER IS A VERY BUSY TIME around a Purple Martin complex. Adults spiral around the large, communal nest box, coming and going from foraging forays. The year's young perch at the opening of their apartment cavity, impatiently waiting for their parents to return with a mouthful of flying insects. A patient observer will notice how orderly the apparent confusion is to the martin, and how efficiently the crowded complex is negotiated.

The fascinating experiences are rewards to residents who erect Purple Martin complexes on their properties. These large apartment complexes are the preferred nesting site for large groups of our biggest swallows, which are communal nesters. Because many of their historic breeding sites have been eliminated by deforestation, Purple Martins, much to the delight of property owners, depend heavily on these specialized housing complexes.

Quick ID: smaller than a robin; deep, glossy blue; pointed wings; forked tail; small bill; **Females and Immatures:** grey underneath and backs are duller.

Size: 20 cm (8 in.)

Habitat: widespread, often near large lakes, limited by nesting sites.

Nest: natural cavities, communal bird houses; mud and grass nest lined with soft material.

Food: flying insects, rarely berries and ground insects.

Foraging: catches insects on the wing.

Voice: rich, robin-like *pew-pew*.

Similar Species: Barn Swallow (p. 87) has a deeply forked tail; Tree Swallow (p. 85) has a white belly; European Starling (p. 109) has a long bill and a short tail.

Notes: Becoming a landlord to a Purple Martin condominium requires a high degree of responsibility. The apartment should be erected high on a pole, in the middle of a large open area. Trees, shrubs, and houses get in the way of these aerial masters so they will avoid complexes that limit their airways. The Purple Martin complex should be cleaned and then plugged up once the swallows have left, until they return in the spring. House Sparrows and starlings recognize the prestigious accommodations of a typical Martin complex and will overthrow the preferred tenant if given a chance.

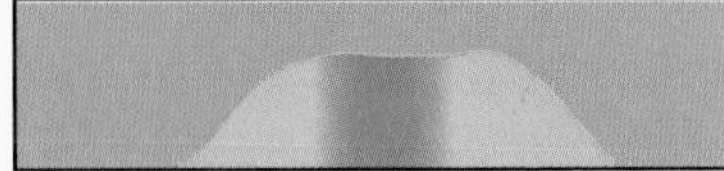

Tree Swallow

Tachycineta bicolor

THE POPULATION OF TREE SWALLOWS has increased during the past decades, as the unforeseen result of a bluebird nest box program. These common swallows are cavity nesters, and are among the most frequent users of nest boxes intended for bluebirds. Tree Swallows compete for the cavities because their own have become so scarce. They choose their nest site after they arrive in early spring, and then enrich their territories with dramatic flight displays.

Natural flyers, swallows spend much of their lives on the wing. They routinely skim low over calm water for a quick drink, leaving only a small wake behind.

Quick ID: sparrow-sized; iridescent blue-green above; white below; long, pointed wings; short tail; sexes similar.

Size: 15 cm (6 in.)

Habitat: open country with neighbouring woodlands, wetlands.

Nest: old woodpecker cavities or nest boxes; of grass and lined with soft materials.

Food: flying insects, berries in early spring (when insects aren't available).

Foraging: catches insects on the wing.

Voice: electrical buzz.

Similar Species: most other swallows lack dark blue-green backs.

Notes: Although most swallows do not generally change colour after molting, the Tree Swallow's back does show a colour shift during its stay in Ontario. In bright sunshine in early spring, the Tree Swallow's back will appear to be blue, while prior to migration in the fall it appears more green. • During fall migration, thousands of swallows congregate in mixed flocks.

Bank Swallow
Riparia riparia

SWALLOWS ARE endlessly enjoyable for a variety of reasons. Their playful flights are wonderful distractions during lazy summer afternoons, and their nesting habits are quite variable. Every swallow seems to have a unique nesting strategy that it alone uses. The Bank Swallow is a colonial cavity nester. Although this strategy is similar to that of the Purple Martin, the Bank Swallow chooses to excavate burrows in stream banks rather than choosing condo-style housing. It is interesting that the Bank Swallow chooses to dig out a burrow, while Barn and Cliff Swallows meticulously form mud nests one mouthful at a time. This diversity in nesting sites ensures that the competition between swallow species is reduced, an advantage for all involved.

Quick ID: larger than a sparrow; grey-brown on back, wings, head, and tail; white underneath; brown chest band; sexes similar.

Size: 17 cm (5 in.)

Habitat: lakes, large rivers, open country, gravel pits.

Food: flying insects.

Foraging: catches insects on the wing.

Nest: colonial burrow; in mud bank or cliff face.

Voice: electrical buzz: *speed-zeet speed-zeet*.

Similar Species: Chimney Swift (p. 69) and Northern Rough-winged Swallow lack a chest band; Tree Swallow (p. 85) has a blue-green back.

Notes: The Northern Rough-winged Swallow occurs in southern Ontario, where it frequently associates with Bank Swallows. These two species are frequently confused, but only the Bank Swallow has a prominent band across its chest. The Northern Rough-winged Swallow often nests in association with a Bank Swallow colony, but they are not limited to these colonial burrows and occasionally choose to nest in culverts and under bridges. • The genus and species name *riparia* means 'shorelines' or 'stream banks.'

Barn Swallow
Hirundo rustica

THE GRACEFUL FLIGHT of these birds is a common summer sight. Barn Swallows build their cup-shaped mud nests in the eaves of barns, picnic shelters, and occasionally in nest boxes or any other structure that provides protection from the rain. Because Barn Swallows are often closely associated with human structures, it is not uncommon for a nervous parent to dive repeatedly at human 'intruders,' forcing them to retreat. Unfortunately, Barn Swallows and their nests are unwanted by many property owners, who find that the mud structure, the aggressive parent, and the droppings detract from their property. This is unfortunate because Barn Swallows are endlessly fascinating and entertaining with their aerial antics.

Quick ID: larger than a sparrow; deeply forked tail; glossy blue back, wings and tail; chestnut underneath; russet throat and forehead; sexes similar but female is a bit duller.

Size: 17 cm (7 in.)

Habitat: widespread; urban areas, farmyards, open country.

Food: flying insects.

Foraging: catches insects on the wing.

Jan Feb Mar Apr May Jun Jul Aug Sept Oct Nov Dec

Nest: mud cup; usually under a ledge in barns, picnic shelters, or on bridges.

Voice: sharp but soft *vit-vit-vit-vit*.

Similar Species: Purple Martins (p. 84) are dark all over; Cliff Swallows lack the deeply forked tail and creamy forehead.

Notes: 'Swallow tail' is a term frequently used to describe something that is deeply forked. This description would seem inappropriate for most Ontario swallows, except for the Barn Swallow. The Barn Swallow is also the common swallow of Europe, from where the phrase 'swallow tail' originates.

Gray Jay

Perisoreus canadensis

WHEN MOST OTHER BIRDS have abandoned the north woods for the winter months, the Gray Jay remains and livens up the short December days. From behind a curtain of spruce, a small flock of curious Gray Jays will investigate the sounds of an intruder. Their appearance is not antagonistic; Gray Jays appear profoundly interested in all life forms that exist within the quiet winter forest. It is impossible to know for certain the reason for the Gray Jay's amicable personality, but it is clear that its friendly behaviour is appreciated by humans. Affectionately known as the Whiskey Jack, Canada Jay, and Camp Robber (among others), the bird's list of nicknames is a testament to our appreciation. Although anyone open to nature can sense the Gray Jay's spirit, birdwatchers are especially indebted to this fluffy character. Previously unheard bird songs that hopeful birders sometimes initially attribute to new or other existing species, are often simply the products of the Gray Jay's diverse vocal repertoire.

Quick ID: Blue Jay-sized; fluffy grey; darker on back wings and tail; light on belly, throat, and forehead; long tail; dark bill; sexes similar; **Immatures:** dark grey overall.

Size: 29 cm (12 in.)

Habitat: northern coniferous forests.

Nest: bulky stick nest lined with fur and feathers; in coniferous trees.

Food: invertebrates, berries, carrion.

Foraging: gleans vegetation, rarely flycatches, stores food.

Voice: variable, often a soft *quee-oo*. If you can't attribute a sound to any other bird, it's probably a Gray Jay!

Similar Species: shrikes are boldly patterned and are black and white; Gray Catbird (p. 105) has a black cap.

Notes: As a bird of the boreal forest, the Gray Jay would be a great candidate for a Canadian national bird. Gray Jays begin to lay their eggs as early as February; their nests are well insulated to maintain heat. This early nesting enables the jays to be feeding the quickly growing nestlings when the forests are in full spring bloom.

• 'Whiskey Jack' is from the Algonquin name for this bird, *Wiskedjack*, and isn't a reflection of its beverage preference. *Perisoreus* is from the Greek word *perisoreyein*, meaning 'to heap up,' and refers to this jay's food-storing habits.

Jan Feb Mar Apr May Jun Jul Aug Sept Oct Nov Dec

Blue Jay
Cyanocitta cristata

SOUTHERN ONTARIO, with its broken forests, plentiful birdfeeders, and relatively easy winters, must look a lot like Blue Jay heaven. One of the region's most identifiable birds, with its loud *jay-jay-jay* call, blue and white plumage, and large crest, it is familiar to anyone with sunflower seeds or peanuts at their birdfeeder.

Blue Jays are intelligent, aggressive birds that don't hesitate to drive smaller birds, squirrels or even cats away when they feel threatened.

The Blue Jay represents all the admirable virtues and aggressive qualities of the corvid family. While it is beautiful, resourceful, and vocally diverse, the Blue Jay can be one of the most annoying and mischievous birds, and no predator is too formidable for this bird to harass. With noisy calls, Blue Jays wake up neighbourhoods and forests where they are the self-appointed guardians, but this colourful bird's extroverted character outweighs its occasional annoying behaviour.

Quick ID: blue crest, back wings, and tail; black necklace; white wing bars; light belly; sexes similar.

Size: 28 cm (11 in.)

Habitat: mixed-wood and deciduous forests, agricultural areas, city parks, backyard feeders.

Nest: bulky stick nest; on branches of conifers or in forks of deciduous trees.

Food: nuts, berries, other birds' eggs and nestlings, invertebrates, carrion, birdseed, especially peanuts.

Foraging: gleans vegetation and ground.

Voice: loud *jay-jay-jay*, occasionally calls like the horn from an old Model-T Ford (*haaaarnk*), also mimics other birds.

Similar Species: unmistakable.

Notes: Although most people think of Ontario when a Blue Jay is mentioned, they are by no means restricted to this area. This widespread bird occurs from Alberta and the Maritimes down through the Gulf states. A highly adaptable species, it continues to expand its range north and west, forever bullying its way onto birdfeeders.

American Crow

Corvus brachyrhynchos

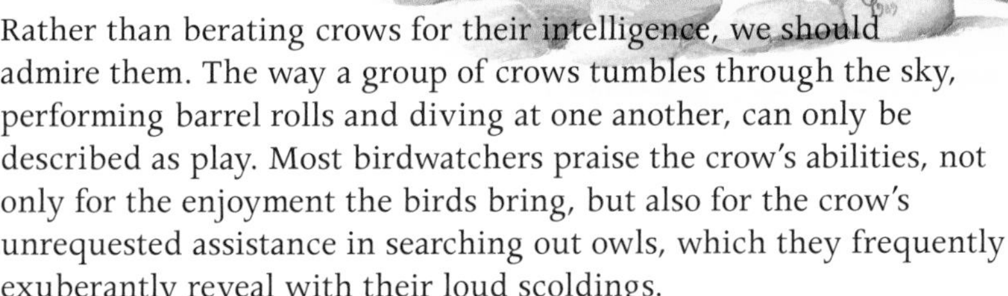

THE AMERICAN CROW is a common sight over much of Ontario. This large blackbird's intelligence has led it into many confrontations with humans, and it often emerges the victor. Scientific analysis of crow behaviour has shown that crows are capable of solving simple problems, which comes as no surprise to the many Ontarians who have watched American Crows systematically search for garbage in sealed containers.

Rather than berating crows for their intelligence, we should admire them. The way a group of crows tumbles through the sky, performing barrel rolls and diving at one another, can only be described as play. Most birdwatchers praise the crow's abilities, not only for the enjoyment the birds bring, but also for the crow's unrequested assistance in searching out owls, which they frequently exuberantly reveal with their loud scoldings.

Quick ID: large crow; black; fan-shaped tail; slim overall; sexes similar.

Size: 45 cm (18 in.)

Habitat: open country, urban areas, shorelines, deciduous forests.

Nest: stick and twig nest lined with fine material; in mature coniferous or deciduous trees.

Food: carrion, small vertebrates, invertebrates, other birds' eggs and nestlings, berries, seeds—almost anything.

Foraging: gleans vegetation and ground.

Voice: distinctive *caw-caw-caw.*

Similar Species: Common Raven (p. 91) is much larger, with a diamond-shaped tail; Common Grackle (p. 135) is smaller, with a longer tail.

Notes: *Corvus brachyrhynchos*, despite sounding cumbersome, simply means 'the raven with the small nose (or beak).' • In the fall when their reproductive duties are completed, American Crows group together in flocks known as a 'murders.' This odd name may not be fair, but with a Hitchcockian flock of several thousand crows not uncommon in Ontario, the term 'murder' is understandable.

Jan Feb Mar Apr May Jun Jul Aug Sept Oct Nov Dec

Common Raven

Corvus corax

THE LARGEST and perhaps the most intelligent of the songbirds has a dignified presence about it. Whether stealing food from under the snout of a bear, harassing a Bald Eagle in mid-air, or confidently strutting among campers at a favourite park, the raven is worthy of its reputation as a clever bird. Glorified in traditional cultures worldwide, ravens are not restricted to the instinctive behaviours of most other birds. With the ability to express themselves playfully, tumbling aimlessly through the air or sliding down a snowy bank on their backs, these large, raucous birds flaunt traits many think of as being exclusively human. By behaving unexpectedly, Common Ravens teach us their greatest lessons, reminding us how little insight we have into the non-human world.

Quick ID: large than a hawk; black; large bill; spade-shaped tail; shaggy throat; primaries spread while soaring; sexes similar.

Size: 61 cm (24 in.)

Habitat: northern forests, shorelines.

Nest: large, of sticks and branches, lined with fur and soft materials; on cliffs, tall conifers, hydro towers.

Food: carrion, small vertebrates, mollusks, other birds' eggs and nestlings, berries—very opportunistic.

Foraging: soaring patrols, gleans ground.

Voice: deep, guttural *craaw-craaw*.

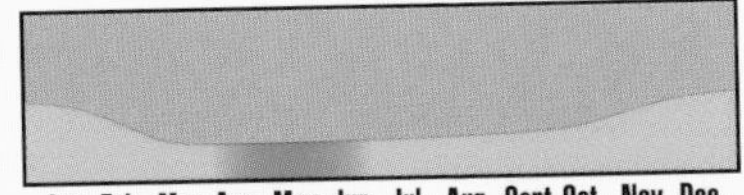

Similar Species: American Crow (p. 90) is much smaller and has a fan-shaped tail; hawks have fan-shaped tails and are not all-black.

Notes: There are few other birds that naturally occur over as large a geographic range as does the Common Raven. From the Mexican desert to the Canadian Arctic and all around the Northern Hemisphere, the raven has always associated with humans. Although poems, folklore, and totems have been erected to honour this great bird, the raven has also fallen victim to indiscriminate slaughter. • In Ontario, the Common Raven continues to recolonize the south from its northern stronghold, and appears increasingly during winter.

Black-capped Chickadee

Parus atricapillus

THE BLACK-CAPPED CHICKADEE is one of the most pleasant birds in our cities and forested areas. This exceptionally friendly bird often greets walkers along trails, welcoming them into the chickadee's world of shrubs, dry leaves, and insect eggs. Throughout most of the year, chickadees move about in loose flocks, investigating their human visitors, surrounding them with their delicate *chick-a-dee-dee-dee* calls.

During the summer, Black-capped Chickadees seem strangely absent from city parks and wooded ravines—they may be too busy raising their families to greet and entertain passersby. It seems that chickadees let flighty migrants have their way in the woods for three brief summer months, but once the first autumn chill arrives, the woods will once again be theirs.

Quick ID: smaller than a sparrow; black cap and bib; white cheek; greyish back wings and tail; light underneath; faint chestnut flanks; sexes similar.

Size: 13 cm (5 in.)

Habitat: deciduous and mixed-wood forests, city parks, backyard feeders.

Nest: natural cavities, old woodpecker holes, nest boxes; lined with fine materials.

Food: invertebrate adults, larvae and eggs, wild-bird seed, berries.

Foraging: gleans vegetation, flycatches.

Voice: call: *chick-a-dee-dee-dee*; song: whistled *swee-tee.*

Similar Species: Boreal Chickadee is common in Northern Ontario and has a grey cap and russet flanks; Blackpoll Warbler is uncommon, has yellow-orange legs, and is slimmer.

Notes: Most songbirds have both songs and calls. Bird songs are delivered primarily during the breeding season to attract mates and to defend a territory. Calls can be heard year-round, as the birds vocalize to establish flock cohesion and contact.

Red-breasted Nuthatch

Sitta canadensis

THIS COMMON, YEAR-ROUND resident of coniferous and mixed-wood forests has a precarious foraging habit. Unlike other birds, which forage moving up tree trunks, nuthatches move down trunks—headfirst. They occasionally stop with their heads held out at a right angle to the trunk. By moving down the tree, Red-breasted Nuthatches are able to find seeds, insects, and nuts that have been overlooked by woodpeckers.

Although the Red-breasted Nuthatch may look somewhat like a woodpecker, its feeding habits, black eyeline, and blue-grey back should eliminate any confusion. Bird feeders in older communities adjacent to mature forests will often attract Red-breasted Nuthatches during winter. Their distinctive, nasal *yank-yank-yank* call is heard increasingly as spring arrives.

Quick ID: smaller than a sparrow; **Male:** red breast; black eyeline; white eyebrow; black cap; steel-blue back, wings, and tail; short tail; **Female:** similar but with a dark-grey cap.

Size: 11 cm (5 in.)

Habitat: coniferous forests, pine plantations.

Nest: cavities in rotting wood, old woodpecker nests, lined with fine materials.

Food: invertebrate adults, larvae and eggs, seeds.

Foraging: probes and hammers bark.

Voice: nasal *yank-yank-yank*.

Similar Species: White-breasted Nuthatch (p. 94) has a white breast; Downy Woodpecker (p. 74) is black and white.

Notes: The nesting cavities of Red-breasted Nuthatches are easily identifiable—this small woodland bird frequently smears the entrance to its nest with sap. The sticky doormat may inhibit ants and other insects from entering the nest chamber and affecting the nestlings. • Although both sexes of the Red-breasted Nuthatch have distinctive red breasts, the male's is more pronounced than the female's.

White-breasted Nuthatch

Sitta carolinensis

THE WHITE-BREASTED NUTHATCH is a curious bird. To the novice birdwatcher, seeing a nuthatch call repeatedly while clinging to the underside of a branch is an odd sight. To nuthatches, this gravity-defying act is as natural as flight is to other birds. Nuthatches frequently pause in mid-descent, arch their heads out at right angles to the trunks and call noisily, making dangerous headfirst hops seem somewhat routine.

White-breasted Nuthatches frequently visit backyard feeders. Nuthatches seem less at home on the level platform feeders, as they cast aside their tree-trunk talent for an easy meal of sunflower seeds.

Quick ID: sparrow-sized; **Male:** black cap; white cheek and breast; steel-blue back, wings and tail; straight bill; short tail; russet undertail coverts; **Female:** similar but with a greyish cap.

Size: 15 cm (6 in.)

Habitat: deciduous forests, urban areas, backyard feeders.

Nest: cavities in rotting wood, old woodpecker nests, lined with fine materials.

Food: invertebrate adults, larvae and eggs, seeds.

Foraging: probes and hammers bark.

Voice: distinctive and often repeated *yarnk-yarnk-yarnk*.

Similar Species: Red-breasted Nuthatch (p. 93) has a red breast and a black eyeline; most woodpeckers have black backs.

Notes: By all rights, the White-breasted Nuthatch should not be capable of hanging onto the vertical surfaces of trees. Unlike woodpeckers and the Brown Creeper, nuthatches do not use their tails for support as braces against the trunks. In fact, their tails are so short they couldn't possibly serve that purpose even in emergency situations. These birds clasp the trunks through foot power alone. • The nuthatches' species names are good indicators of habitat: *canadensis* ('of Canada') refers to northern coniferous forests and *carolinensis* ('of the Carolinas') pertains to southern deciduous forests.

Brown Creeper
Certhia americana

THE BROWN CREEPER may be the most inconspicuous bird in North America. Embracing the trees of old coniferous forests, Creepers often go unnoticed until a flake of bark seems to come alive. Short, purposeful, vertical hops enable the Brown Creeper to spiral up the rugged trunks while constantly probing the tree's wrinkled skin for hidden invertebrate treasures.

When the spiral has reached the upper branches, the tiny bird floats down to the base of a neighbouring tree to resume its grooming ascent. Only during their brief flights are Brown Creepers easily noticed, as even their thin, high-pitched whistle is too high for many birders to actually hear and rarely reveals this master of concealment.

Quick ID: smaller than a sparrow; brown back streaked with white; white breast; rusty rump; downcurved bill; long tail; sexes similar.

Size: 13 cm (5 in.)

Habitat: mature coniferous or mixed-wood forests, moist woods.

Nest: grass, spruce needles woven with spider silk; under loose bark.

Food: invertebrate adults, larvae and eggs, seeds.

Jan Feb Mar Apr May Jun Jul Aug Sept Oct Nov Dec

Foraging: probes and hammers bark.

Voice: faint, high-pitched *trees trees trees see the trees.*

Similar Species: Black and White Warbler is black and white; wrens generally hold their tails cocked up.

Notes: Like woodpeckers, Brown Creepers brace themselves against tree trunks with their stiff tails. • Although there are numerous creepers in Europe and Asia, the Brown Creeper is the only North American representative. • The Brown Creeper's abundance is underestimated because of its cryptic habits; however, a diligent search of a coniferous stand will often yield a rewarding view.

House Wren
Troglodytes aedon

THIS COMMON BIRD OF SUBURBS, city parks, and woodlands sings as though its lungs were bottomless. The sweet, warbling song of the House Wren is distinguished by its melodious tone and its uninterrupted endurance. Although the House Wren is far smaller than a sparrow, it offers an unending song in one breath.

Like all wrens, the House Wren frequently carries its short tail cocked straight up. This bird is often observed in woodlands, city parks, and backyards, skulking beneath the dense understorey from May to September. As spring arrives, the House Wren treats Ontarians to a few weeks of wonderful warbles, and then channels its energy into the task of reproduction.

Quick ID: smaller than a sparrow; brown; tail often cocked up; bill slightly downcurved; tail as long as legs; sexes similar.

Size: 12 cm (5 in.)

Habitat: thickets, shrubby areas, urban parks and backyards.

Nest: of twigs and grass; often in cavities or tight places, nest boxes.

Food: adult and larval invertebrates.

Foraging: gleans vegetation, flycatches.

Voice: flowing, bubbly warble, frequently lasting 3 seconds or more.

Similar Species: Winter Wren has cinnamon plumage, and its tail is shorter than its legs; Carolina Wren has a white eyebrow.

Notes: *Troglodytes aedon* is Greek for 'a songster who creeps in holes' and is a wonderful description of this small bird. • The Winter Wren of northern Ontario has a song that surpasses the House Wren in quality and endurance. The Winter Wren (*T. troglodytes*) of the boreal forest is also the only European wren; it is the one often revered in English literature.

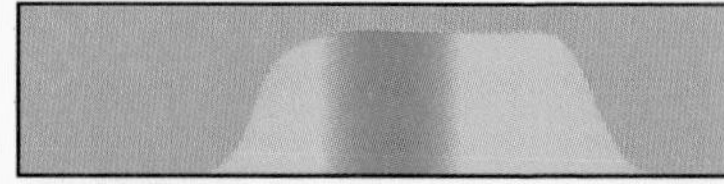

Marsh Wren

Cistothorus palustris

THIS ENERGETIC LITTLE BIRD is usually associated with dense cattail marshes. Although it prefers to keep a low profile by staying hidden in the deep vegetation, its distinctive song is one of the characteristic voices of our wetlands. The song of this small, streaked bird has the repetitive quality of an old sewing machine. Once you learn the rhythm, you will be unable to avoid hearing it when you visit suitable Marsh Wren habitats.

A typical sighting of a Marsh Wren is usually nothing more than spotting a brown blur moving noisily about deep within the cattails. Although the wren may be less than three metres (10 ft.) from the observer, its cryptic habits and appearance are frustratingly effective camouflage. Patient observers may be rewarded with a brief glimpse of a Marsh Wren perching high atop a cattail reed as it quickly evaluates its territory.

Quick ID: smaller than a sparrow; brown overall; white streaking on back; white eyeline; light throat and breast; cocked-up tail; sexes similar.

Size: 13 cm (5 in.)

Habitat: cattail and bulrush marshes.

Nest: melon-sized globe woven with grasses and cattail down, circular side entrance; in cattails.

Food: aquatic insects, occasionally mollusks, other invertebrates.

Foraging: gleans vegetation and substrate, flycatches.

Voice: a quick series of *zig-zig-zig-zig*, like an old sewing machine.

Similar Species: House Wren (p. 96) has an unstreaked back; Sedge Wren lacks prominent white eyeline, and is usually found in wet meadows.

Notes: Although the Marsh Wren is difficult to see, its song is one of the easiest to identify. • During cold winter days, search frozen cattail marshes for abandoned Marsh Wren nests. • The Sedge Wren prefers wet meadows to cattails; it can be distinguished from the Marsh Wren by its song.

Golden-crowned Kinglet

Regulus satrapa

THE HIGH-PITCHED, TINKLING VOICE of the Golden-crowned Kinglet is as familiar as the sweet smell of spruce and fir in coniferous forests. Although not immediately obvious to the uninformed passerby, a birdwatcher with a keen ear, patience, and the willingness to draw down this smallest of North American songbirds with squeaks and pishes will encounter kinglets on many outdoor trips.

As these tiny birds descend in loose flocks toward the curious noise, their indistinct plumage and voice offer little excitement. It is when the flock circles about the noise, using the branches as swings and trapezes, flashing their regal crowns, that the magic of the kinglet emerges.

Quick ID: smaller than a sparrow; plump; dark olive; white wing bars; dark tail and wings; white eyebrow; **Male:** fiery orange crown bordered by black; **Female:** lemon-yellow crown bordered by black.

Size: 10 cm (4 in.)

Habitat: mature coniferous forests (often spruce, pine, fir, hemlock), conifer plantations.

Nest: hung from a high spruce branch; woven with grass, spider silk, moss.

Food: small invertebrates.

Foraging: gleans vegetation, flycatches.

Voice: faint, high-pitched, accelerating *tsee-tsee-tsee-tsee, why do you shilly-shally?*

Similar Species: Ruby-crowned Kinglet, common in Northern Ontario, lacks black outline to the crown; warblers generally are more colourful or lack a crown.

Notes: Ruby-crowned Kinglets are also very common in Ontario's coniferous forests. They are similar in size, habits, and colouration to the Golden-crowned Kinglets, but they have a hidden ruby crown. 'Rubies' are heard far more often then they are seen. Their song starts like a motor chugging to life, and then they fire off a series of *chewy-chewy-chewy-chewy* that rises at the end. The final phrases are often the only recognizable part of the song.

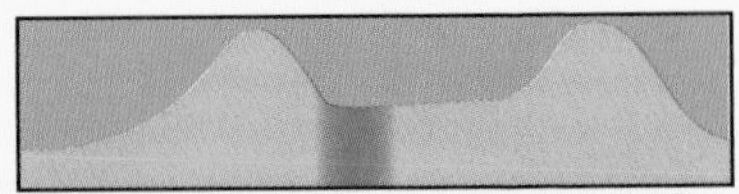

Eastern Bluebird

Sialia sialis

DRESSED WITH THE COLOURS of the cool sky on its back and the warm setting sun on its chest, the male Eastern Bluebird looks like a piece of pure sky come to life. To fully appreciate this open-country specialty, try to spot a male as he sets up his territory on a crisp, early spring morning.

The Eastern Bluebird lost many of its natural nesting sites in vacant cavities to House Sparrows and European Starlings, and to the removal of dead trees from Ontario. But concerned residents rallied for this bird, and put up thousands of nesting boxes to compensate for the losses. The Eastern Bluebird population has slowly increased as a result, and the vigilant residents have been rewarded with the sight of the birds' beautiful plumage.

Quick ID: smaller than a robin; sky-blue back; red throat and breast; white undertail coverts; thin bill; **Female:** less intense blue.

Size: 18 cm (7 in.)

Habitat: open areas including pastures, forest clearings, golf courses, agricultural areas.

Nest: abandoned woodpecker cavities or nest boxes; loose bowl of grass and other vegetation.

Food: flying insects, earthworms, berries.

Foraging: flycatches, gleans vegetation.

Voice: common call: *chur-lee;* song: *cheer cheerful charmer.*

Similar Species: American Robin (p. 103) has a dark back; male Indigo Bunting (p. 123) lacks red breast and has a conical bill.

Notes: The comeback of the Eastern Bluebird has been slow, and in many areas of apparently suitable bluebird habitat there are far more bluebird nest boxes than there are bluebirds. This only accentuates the small positive occurences that undoubtably happen each year—like when a new one sets up territory. There is a well-established system of bluebird-box trails, but continuing to erect the boxes is never a waste of time.

Veery

Catharus fuscescens

LIKE A TUMBLING WATERFALL, the Veery's voice descends with a liquid ripple. This bird, like all other thrushes, is a master of melodies, and offers its unequalled songs to dusky forests.

The Veery is perhaps the most terrestrial of Ontario's thrushes; it frequently nests on the ground. In characteristic thrush style, the Veery searches for grubs and caterpillars by shuffling through loose leaf-litter. When an invertebrate delicacy is found, it is swallowed quickly, and the ever-vigilant Veery cautiously looks about before renewing the hunt.

Quick ID: smaller than a robin; reddish-brown head, back, rump, and tail; faint spotting on throat; no eye-ring; sexes similar.

Size: 20 cm (8 in.)

Habitat: dense undergrowth in moist decidous or mixed-wood forests.

Nest: on ground or in shrubs close to ground; bulky bowl made of grass, twigs, and other vegetation.

Food: invertebrates, berries.

Foraging: gleans ground and vegetation, flycatches.

Voice: musical, tumbling spiral.

Similar Species: Wood (p. 102), Hermit (p. 101), and Swainson's Thrushes are more boldly patterned on the breast.

Notes: Wherever in Ontario one ventures during the summer, the songs of thrushes resound. The Eastern Bluebird patrols open fields, while the robin graces cities and forests. In mature forests, one can hear the songs of Veery and of Wood, Swainson's, and Hermit Thrushes, each segregated to areas of specific forest age and composition. In the far north where forest and tundra meet, the Gray-cheeked Thrush enlivens the landscape with its musical talent.

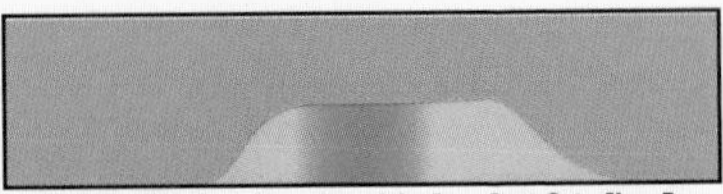

Hermit Thrush
Catharus guttatus

BEAUTY IN FOREST BIRDS is often gauged by sound and not appearance. Given this criterion, the Hermit Thrush is certainly one of the most beautiful birds to inhabit Ontario woodlands. A migrant to boreal forests, Hermit Thrushes are heard but rarely seen during their all too brief four-month stay, revealing themselves mainly when flocking together for the southern migration.

The upward spiral in the song of the Hermit Thrush lifts the soul with each note, and leaves a fortunate listener breathless at its conclusion. The inspiring song is heard in early spring mornings, but is most appreciated at dusk, when the Hermit Thrush alone offers a melody to the darkening forest.

Quick ID: smaller than a robin; rusty-red rump and tail; olive-brown head and back; light eye-ring; olive-brown spots on upper chest; light underneath; sexes similar.

Size: 19 cm (8 in.)

Habitat: northern forests, including mixed-wood forests, and spruce bogs.

Nest: often on the ground or low in trees; bowl of twigs and moss with a layer of mud.

Food: invertebrates, earthworms, spiders, berries.

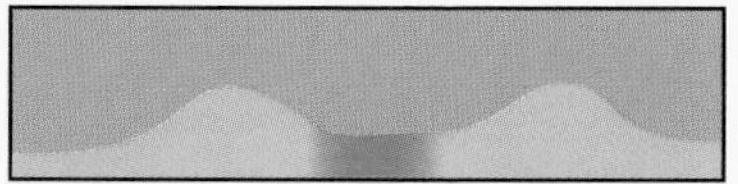

Foraging: gleans ground and vegetation.

Voice: warbling upward spiral, always preceded by a lone, thin note.

Similar Species: Swainson's Thrush; Wood Thrush (p. 102); Veery (p. 100); all lack red rump and tail and olive back.

Notes: The identification of thrushes is always confusing to novice birdwatchers. The features of the Hermit Thrush can be remembered by association with this bird's name. Its memorable song always begins with a single, lone (hermit-like) note. The lower back and tail of this thrush is red, which reminds me of a lonely old hermit walking around wearing nothing but a pair of red long underwear.

Wood Thrush
Hylocichla mustelina

THE FLUTE-LIKE SONG that accompanied and inspired the tireless work of Ontario's pioneers is slowly fading away. The Wood Thrush was once the voice of eastern hardwood forests, but it is one of the birds most sensitive to forest fragmentation. As the forests disappeared, their songster followed their path toward silence. Broken forests invite common predators such as the skunk, fox, crow, and jay, which traditionally had no access to the Wood Thrush nests insulated deep within the protected confines of vast hardwoods. Cowbirds, historically linked to the open prairies, now parasitize the unknowing thrush's nests, depositing foreign eggs within its brood (see p. 136).

Like the hope and faith that seem to flow with the Wood Thrush melody, the future may still hold promise for this often-glorified songbird. As the pioneer farms are slowly abandoned and society learns to value the sanctity of a bird song, the wild spirit of the Wood Thrush offers up an optimistic note.

Quick ID: smaller than a robin; large black spots on white breast; reddish-brown head; brown rump and tail; white eye-ring; plump; sexes similar.

Size: 21 cm (8 in.)

Habitat: mature deciduous or mixed-wood forests, preferably moist and unfragmented.

Nest: usually in mature deciduous trees; bulky bowl made of vegetation with a middle layer of mud.

Food: flying insects, spiders, berries.

Foraging: gleans vegetation and ground.

Voice: musical warble: *Will you live with me? Way up high in a tree, I'll come right down and...seeee;* or a series of *ee-o-lay.*

Similar Species: Hermit Thrush (p. 101); Veery (p. 100); Swainson's Thrush; all lack bold black chest spots and reddish head.

Notes: As the 'poster child' of the eastern forest-fragmentation research campaign, the Wood Thrush's population declines are frequently quoted in scientific investigations. It would suit the bird's dignity more if it were the Wood Thrush's song that would gain reverence, and not its sad plight in the face of habitat destruction.

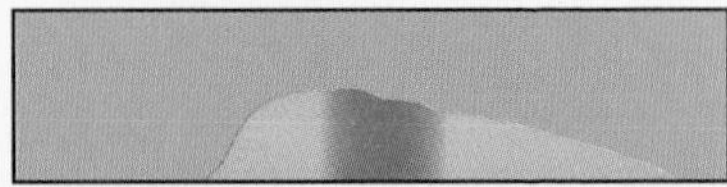

American Robin

Turdus migratorius

THE ROBIN is much more than a common backyard bird with a flute-like voice. Many Ontarians anxiously await its annual March arrival, as if the return of this distinctive bird injects them with the energy needed to withstand the final weeks of winter. The robin's close relationship with urban areas has allowed many humans an insight into a bird's social and ecological role. A robin dashing around a yard in search of worms or ripe berries is as familiar to many people as is its three-part song. Robins make up part of the emotional landscape of communities, as their song, their young's hatching and fast development, and occasionally even their deaths, are experiences shared by their human neighbours.

Quick ID: smaller than a Blue Jay; brick-red breast (female's slightly more orange); dark head, back, and tail; white undertail coverts; **Male:** has a darker hood.

Size: 25 cm (10 in.)

Habitat: widespread, from backyards and city parks to mixed-wood forests, prefers forests with openings.

Nest: in shrubs, trees, and on ledges; shaggy bowl of mud and grasses.

Food: invertebrates, berries.

Foraging: gleans ground and vegetation.

Voice: song: evenly spaced warble, *cheerily-cheery up-cheerio*; call: *tut-tut-tut.*

Similar Species: immature robins can be confused with other thrushes, but robins always have at least a hint of red in the breast.

Notes: Some people erroneously place bird houses in their backyards to encourage a nesting pair of American Robins. Unfortunately, robins do not choose nest boxes, but prefer open platforms, usually those placed upon buildings. Although American Robins quite willingly choose to nest in backyards with shrubs and dense trees to provide cover, a special platform will attract a pair to a yard otherwise free of nesting cover.

Black-billed Cuckoo

Coccyzus erythropthalmus

ALTHOUGH BLACK-BILLED CUCKOOS MIGRATE to and from South and Central America, they seem to avoid long flights while in Ontario. In their dense, tangled habitat, cuckoos are difficult to find, revealing themselves only occasionally to make a direct low flight to an undisturbed hideout.

Ontario's cuckoos do not sing in the cuckoo-clock tradition; that voice is from a European relative. The Black-billed Cuckoo is not musical, but what it lacks in tone it makes up for in delivery. Its loud call is fired off in bursts from thickets at night or preceding storms. The frequency and intensity of the evening chorus escalates in some years, when the population of Black-billed Cuckoos rises in response to outbreaks of tent caterpillars.

Quick ID: pigeon-sized; long tail; olive-brown above, pale below; downturned black bill; reddish eye-ring; sexes similar.

Size: 31 cm (12 in.)

Habitat: dense, shrubby areas near open areas.

Nest: loose twig nest, lined with fine plant material; on limb or log.

Food: mainly hairy caterpillars, some berries, small invertebrates.

Foraging: gleans vegetation and ground.

Voice: raspy *cu-cu-cu*, in 3s and 4s.

Similar Species: Mourning Dove (p. 66) is white on tail; Yellow-billed Cuckoo is rufous-coloured on wings, has white spots on tail and a yellow eye-ring; Sharp-shinned Hawk (p. 43) has a hooked bill, longer legs and a streaked breast.

Notes: Although most cuckoos raise their own young, some lay their eggs in the nests of other songbirds instead. This brood parasitism often results in the foster parents raising the young cuckoos at the expense of their own, slower-growing offspring. Although this is damaging to individual songbirds, the practice is not so widespread that it threatens certain songbird populations.

Jan Feb Mar Apr May Jun Jul Aug Sept Oct Nov Dec

Gray Catbird
Dumetella carolinensis

THE GRAY CATBIRD is a sleek bird that commonly displays an unusual 'mooning' behaviour: it raises its long, slender tail to show its chestnut undertail coverts. This behaviour is one of the elements of courtship, and the coverts may help female catbirds to choose the best mates.

The Gray Catbird is a bird of dense shrubs and thickets, and although it's relatively common in appropriate habitats, its distinctive call, rather than the bird itself, is what is most commonly encountered. The Gray Catbird's unmistakable cat-like 'meowing,' for which it's named, is the key to field (or city) identification.

Quick ID: robin-sized; slate-grey; black cap; chestnut undertail coverts; long, dark tail; sexes similar.

Size: 23 cm (9 in.)

Habitat: thickets in valleys, rural areas, hedgerows.

Nest: bulky bowl of twigs and other vegetation; usually in dense shrubs.

Food: insects, other invertebrates, berries.

Foraging: gleans ground and vegetation.

Voice: song: variable warbles, usually in pairs; call: cat-like *meoow*.

Similar Species: Gray Jay (p. 88); Northern Mockingbird; Loggerhead Shrike (p. 108); all lack chestnut coverts and black cap.

Notes: *Dumetella* is Latin for 'a thicket,' quite appropriate for a bird that inhabits dense tangles. • This bird's call confuses many people, who mistake the bird for a feline friend. Relatively common, the Gray Catbird is a bird many birdwatchers can meet with just a little experience, despite this bird's shrubby habitat. • During fall migration, many night-flying catbirds fatally strike towers and tall buildings.

Brown Thrasher

Toxostoma rufum

MALE BROWN THRASHERS have the largest vocal repertoire of any Ontario bird—more than 3,000 song types. Although thrashers don't have the sweetest voice in Ontario, their loud, continually varying songs are worth a listen. Thrashers will repeat phrases twice, often combining them into complex choruses.

Brown Thrashers have a reddish-brown back and tail and a heavily streaked breast. They're common in thickets and shrubs, often in close proximity to humans. They're shy birds, and they need a lot of coaxing with squeaks and pishes before they will come out into the open.

Quick ID: Blue Jay-sized; reddish-brown head, back, and tail; heavy chest streaking; long, decurved bill; white wing bars; long tail; no eye-ring; sexes similar.

Size: 29 cm (12 in.)

Habitat: thickets and woodland edges, hedgerows in rural areas.

Nest: often on ground or in dense thickets; of leaves and twigs lined with fine vegetation.

Food: insects, other invertebrates, berries, small vertebrates, seeds.

Foraging: gleans ground and vegetation.

Voice: variable repeating phrases; *dig-it dig-it, hoe-it hoe-it, pull-it-up pull-it-up.*

Similar Species: Wood Thrush (p. 102); Veery (p. 100); both have shorter tails and a straight bill.

Notes: The Brown Thrasher, Gray Catbird, and Northern Mockingbird belong to a family known as 'the mimics' (Mimidae). Although many other bird species imitate sounds (starlings and jays, for example), the mimics are famous for this ability. • Thrashers constitute a diverse family in North America, but most members are confined to the southwestern states.

Cedar Waxwing
Bombycilla cedrorum

A FAINT, HIGH-PITCHED TRILL is often your first clue that waxwings are around. Search the tree tops and these cinnamon-crested birds will serve up a pleasant visual reward as they dart out in quick bursts, snacking on flying insects.

The Cedar Waxwing's body feathers are so fine that they're nearly indistinguishable from one another. Cedar Waxwings are most often seen in large flocks in late summer, when they congregate on fruit trees and quickly eat all the berries. A few Ontarians can remember these visits not only for the birds' singular beauty, but because occasionally the fermentation of the fruit rendered the flock flightless from intoxication. Cedar Waxwings are gentle birds, and the suspicious-looking black mask in no way represents their inoffensive character. During harsh winters, southern Ontario is often visited by Bohemian Waxwings, a large cousin of the Cedar Waxwing.

Quick ID: smaller than a robin; fine, pale brown plumage; small crest; black mask; yellow belly wash; yellow terminal tail band; light undertail coverts; shiny red droplets on wingtips; sexes similar.

Size: 20 cm (8 in.)

Habitat: open decidous and mixed-wood forests, city parks, second-growth forests.

Nest: in conifer or deciduous tree; grass, moss and twig bowl.

Food: flying insects, other invertebrates, berries.

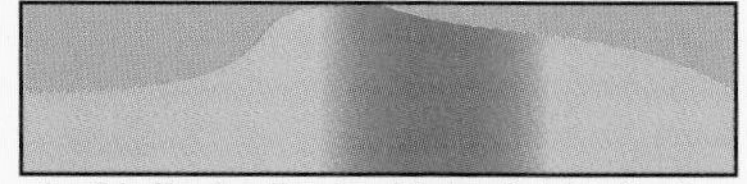

Foraging: gleans vegetation, flycatches.

Voice: high-pitched, faint *tseee tseee.*

Similar Species: Bohemian Waxwings are slightly larger, with chestnut undertail coverts and red and yellow droplets on wingtips.

Notes: In Ontario, many closely related birds show a marked north-south separation in their range. Like the Cedar Waxwing (which breeds primarily in the south), and the Bohemian Waxwing (which breeds primarily in the north), the Black-capped and Boreal Chickadees, White-breasted and Red-Breasted Nuthatches, and House and Winter Wrens all are segregated by changing forest types along a north-south gradient.

Loggerhead Shrike
Lanius ludovicianus

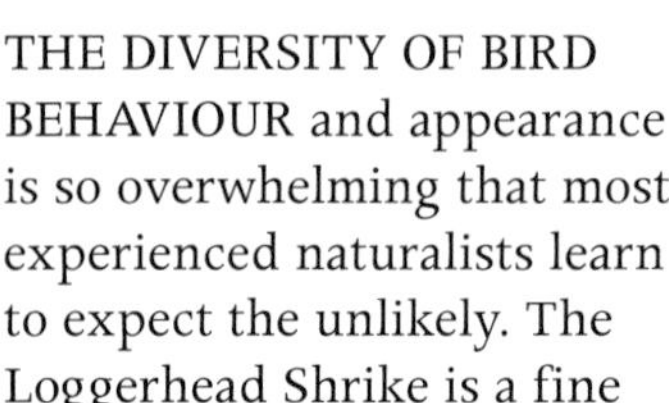

THE DIVERSITY OF BIRD BEHAVIOUR and appearance is so overwhelming that most experienced naturalists learn to expect the unlikely. The Loggerhead Shrike is a fine example of the unexpected—its unassuming appearance gives no clue to its odd habits. Although about the same size as a robin and equipped with similar physical features, shrikes are voracious carnivores, capable of killing mice and small birds. While the finely hooked bill could lead an attentive naturalist to guess the bird's predatory habits, nothing prepares a person for its macabre behaviour. Following a spring kill, male Loggerheads frequently impale their prey (often while it's still alive) onto sharp objects such as thorns or barbed wire, and leave it hanging there. One of the reasons Loggerheads do this is to prove their worth to potential mates.

Quick ID: smaller than a robin; black mask passes over the bill; dark grey crown and back; black wings and tail show white patches in flight; light throat and belly; hooked bill; sexes similar.

Size: 23 cm (9 in.)

Habitat: open country, rough pasture with nearby hedgerows or shrubs.

Nest: bulky twig nest; usually in a dense shrub or thicket.

Food: small mammals, small birds, invertebrates.

Foraging: swoops from a perch, aerial pursuit, flycatches.

Voice: bouncy hiccup, *hugh-ee, hugh-ee*.

Similar Species: Northern Shrikes are uncommon during summer, they have barring on their flanks and no black above the bill.

Notes: Shrikes are also known as 'butcher birds.' • Loggerhead Shrikes are in serious peril in Ontario. Agricultural practices and the conversion of natural grassland to agricultural areas have led to a steady decline in the numbers of this facinating bird. The population continues to be monitored by wildlife officials, but it is unlikely that Ontario's Loggerheads will recover to their former abundance. • Northern Shrikes nest in extreme northern Ontario, and pass through during migration. Although both shrikes look very similar, the Northern Shrike is the only one likely to be seen during the winter months.

Jan Feb Mar Apr May Jun Jul Aug Sept Oct Nov Dec

European Starling
Sturnus vulgaris

SIXTY EUROPEAN STARLINGS were released in New York's Central Park in 1890, as part of the New York Shakespearean Society's plan to introduce to their city all the birds mentioned in their favourite author's plays. The next year, these birds nested (quite ironically) on the American Museum of Natural History. The successful fledging of European Starlings, coupled with the rapid dispersal of the original birds, has altered many elements of natural history in North America. Starlings are continually expanding their range at the expense of native birds, and are now the most common bird in many areas of southern Ontario. The increase in starlings has undoubtably contributed to the decline of a few birds, such as the Eastern Bluebird and some woodpeckers.

These highly adaptable birds, which are often confused with blackbirds, have short tails, and a bright yellow bill to complement their iridiscent breeding plumage. Starlings are accomplished mimics, and can confuse birdwatchers by imitating the calls of many of the species with which they associate.

Quick ID: smaller than a robin; short tail; **breeding:** dark, glossy; long, yellow bill; **non-breeding:** dark bill; spotty plumage; sexes similar.

Size: 21 cm (8 in.)

Habitat: widespread in cities, agricultural areas, open forests.

Nest: natural cavity or nest box; bowl of twigs and fine vegetation.

Jan Feb Mar Apr May Jun Jul Aug Sept Oct Nov Dec

Food: insects, other invertebrates, berries, seeds.

Foraging: gleans ground and vegetation.

Voice: variable; whistles, clicks, imitates.

Similar Species: all blackbirds have long tails and black bills; Purple Martin (p. 84) has a short bill.

Notes: European Starlings apparently weren't held in the highest regard in Europe either. *Sturnus vulgaris* means 'an ordinary and commonplace starling,' which is an appropriate description of the bird in 18th-century Europe and in present-day North America and Europe.

Warbling Vireo

Vireo gilvus

THE WARBLING VIREO'S MUSICAL WARBLE provokes a prolonged search of tree tops. The often-repeated song delights the listening forest with its oscillating quality; the phrases finish on an upbeat, as if asking a question of the wilds. Exceeded in singing endurance only by its Red-eyed cousin, the Warbling Vireo often sings throughout the day, filling spring days with never-ending limericks.

In contrast to its velvety voice, the plumage of this migrant is far less extravagant. Lacking any splashy field marks to complement its voice, the Warbling Vireo appears to hide from view, as if embarrassed by its plain appearance. Searching the high trees as they echo with song frequently produces only a glance of this vireo, as it dances from one leaf-hidden stage to another.

Quick ID: sparrow-sized; grey back; light below; no prominent crown; no eyeline; no wing bars; sexes similar.

Size: 15 cm (6 in.)

Habitat: mature deciduous forests of maple and poplar.

Nest: suspended from a fork; of grasses and fine vegetation.

Food: insects, berries.

Foraging: gleans vegetation.

Voice: repetitive, oscillating and variable warble *I love you, I love you ma'am.*

Similar Species: Red-eyed Vireo (p. 111) has a prominent white eyebrow; Tennessee Warbler has a grey head and green back.

Notes: Ontario is blessed and cursed with vireos. With six easily confused species, Ontario naturalists are continually challenged by the similarity in many vireo songs and plumages. There is no other place in North America with such vireo diversity.

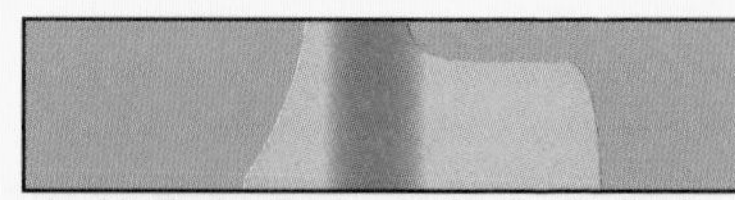

Red-eyed Vireo

Vireo olivaceus

THE RED-EYED VIREO is the undisputed champion of singing endurance. During breeding season, males sing from tall deciduous trees throughout the day. Most songbirds stop their courting melodies five or six hours after sunrise, but the Red-eyed Vireo seems to gain momentum as the day progresses. One patient ornithologist estimated that the energetic Red-eyed Vireo sings its memorable phrase 10,000 to 20,000 times a day.

Visual identification of the Red-eyed Vireo is much harder, since its olive-brown colour conceals it well among the foliage of deciduous trees. Although this vireo does indeed have red eyes, they can only be seen through powerful binoculars in excellent light conditions.

Quick ID: sparrow-sized; grey crown bordered by black; white eyebrow; green back; white underparts; red eye; sexes similar.

Size: 16 cm (6 in.)

Habitat: deciduous and mixed-wood forests.

Nest: suspended from a tree fork; of grasses and fine plant matter.

Food: invertebrates, some berries.

Foraging: gleans vegetation, occasionally hovers.

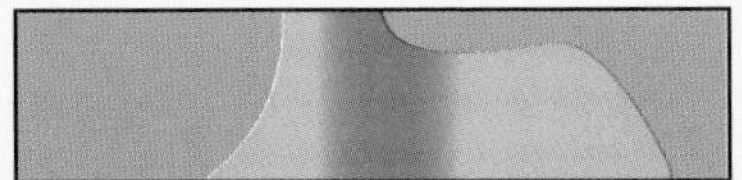

Voice: robin-like quality, distinctive: *look up, way up, tree top, see me, here-I-am.*

Similar Species: Tennessee Warbler; Warbling (p. 110), Philadelphia, and Solitary Vireos; all lack white eyebrow and grey crown.

Notes: All vireos nest in similar fashion. When all the leaves have fallen in the autumn, abandoned vireo nests can be seen suspended from horizontal branch forks high in trees. • The Philadelphia Vireo is fairly common in Ontario and sings very much like a Red-eyed Vireo (in fact, all but the best experts have trouble telling them apart by song), which always raises a sliver of doubt in auditory identifications.

Nashville Warbler

Vermivora ruficapilla

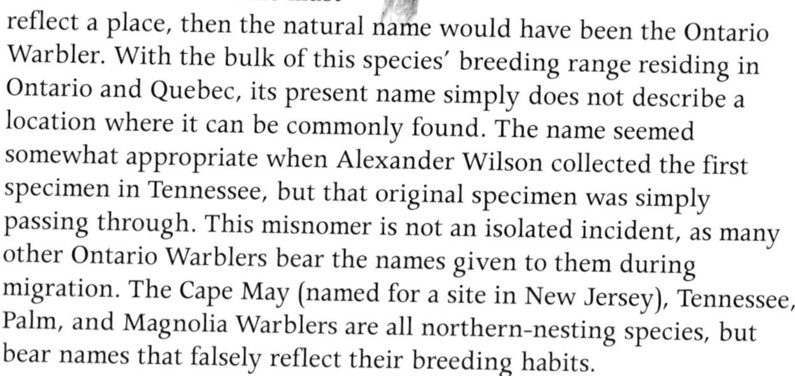

THIS COMMON WARBLER has an identity crisis, not so much a result of its unassuming attire but rather its misleading name. If this small bird's name must reflect a place, then the natural name would have been the Ontario Warbler. With the bulk of this species' breeding range residing in Ontario and Quebec, its present name simply does not describe a location where it can be commonly found. The name seemed somewhat appropriate when Alexander Wilson collected the first specimen in Tennessee, but that original specimen was simply passing through. This misnomer is not an isolated incident, as many other Ontario Warblers bear the names given to them during migration. The Cape May (named for a site in New Jersey), Tennessee, Palm, and Magnolia Warblers are all northern-nesting species, but bear names that falsely reflect their breeding habits.

Quick ID: smaller than a sparrow; yellow underparts from chin through undertail coverts; pale grey head and face; dark olive back; white eye-ring; sexes similar.

Size: 13 cm (5 in.)

Habitat: second-growth, mixed-wood forests.

Nest: on ground; cup of grass and bark.

Food: almost entirely adult and larval insects.

Foraging: gleans vegetation and ground, occasionally hovers.

Voice: starting high then tailing off: *see-it see-it see-it, tee-tee-tee-tee-tee.*

Similar Species: Common Yellowthroat (p. 119) has a black mask; Mourning and Connecticut Warblers have dark grey hood; Yellow Warbler has no grey on head.

Notes: Scientists have been unable to fully explain all the intricacies of migrating birds. One of the many elements birds use to orient themselves is the light from the stars and the moon. Because most warblers migrate at night, they are disoriented by the bright lights of city office towers. During peak migratory periods, thousands of warblers die by crashing into lit windows.

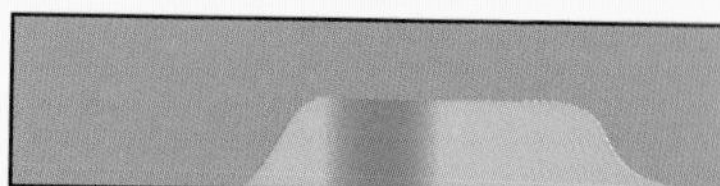

Yellow Warbler
Dendroica petechia

ALTHOUGH THE YELLOW WARBLER is common in shrublands (especially those near water), a glimpse of one is always a sweet surprise. The male—one of the birds frequently and inaccurately called a wild canary—has brilliant yellow plumage that contrasts sharply with his fine red chest streaks.

Adding to the appeal of the Yellow Warbler is its lively courtship song. As one of the most distinctive voices, the Yellow Warbler song is easily recognized in early May despite its nine-month absence. When parasitized by cowbirds (see p. 136), Yellow Warblers will either abandon their nests (like many other birds) or will simply build another nest over the eggs. In true warbler fashion, the Yellow Warbler is active and inquisitive, flitting from branch to branch in search of juicy caterpillars, aphids, and beetles.

Quick ID: smaller than a sparrow; yellow overall; darker back, wings, and tail; dark eye and bill; fine red streaking on breast; **Female:** lacks red streaking.

Size: 13 cm (5 in.)

Habitat: widespread, forest edges, city parks, shrubs.

Nest: compact cup of grasses and fine plant materials.

Food: insects, some berries.

Foraging: gleans vegetation, occasionally hovers.

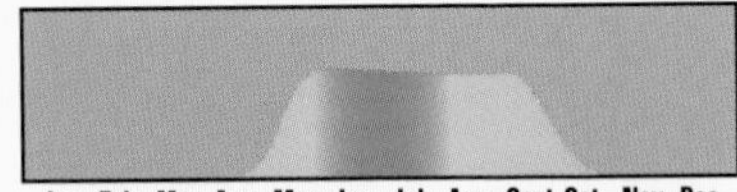

Voice: *sweet sweet sweet, I'm so-so sweet.*

Similar Species: Orange-crowned, Prothonotary, Pine, Wilson's, and Hooded Warblers all lack uniform, overall yellow plumage and red streaks on breast.

Notes: The Yellow Warbler is widely distributed throughout North America, and its appearance varies with its distribution. On islands in Central and South America, Yellow Warblers are non-migratory and have different appearances. While the continental race has red only on its breast, offshore Yellow Warblers can have red on their faces, crowns, and flanks.

Chestnut-sided Warbler

Dendroica pensylvanica

DROPPING DOWN TO HUMAN EYE-LEVEL, the curious Chestnut-sided Warbler invites all into young deciduous stands with a hearty greeting. This common woodland warbler appears genuinely hospitable, as its flitty behaviour often passes within one branch of onlookers. Its distinctive chestnut and white belly accentuate the pleasant experience.

Chestnut-sided Warblers are now among the most common warblers in Ontario. Young, re-growing forests were far less common before colonization than they are today. Because of this change, it is now possible to see more Chestnut-sided Warblers in a single day than some of the great pioneering naturalists saw in their entire lives.

Quick ID: smaller than a sparrow; white underparts with chestnut flanks; yellow crown; white cheek; light wing bars; back dark and mottled; sexes similar.

Size: 13 cm (5 in.)

Habitat: second-growth deciduous forests, shrubby areas.

Nest: in shrubs; small cup of grasses and plant materials.

Food: insects, occasionally berries.

Foraging: gleans vegetation, occasionally hovers.

Voice: *so pleased pleased pleased to meet-cha.*

Similar Species: Bay-breasted, Magnolia, Cape May and other warblers lack white cheek and white throat.

Notes: When the great systematist Linnaeus (1707–78) described the Chestnut-sided Warbler, he gave it the species name *pennsylvanica* ('pennsylvania')—or at least he meant to. Because of a spelling error in the original description of this warbler (he left out an 'n' and spelled it *pensylvanica*), the species name of the Chestnut-sided Warbler must be misspelled to be correct. We should forgive Linneaus for *pensylvanica*: he described hundred of plants and animals, and his binomial classification system is used today, as it has been for over 200 years.

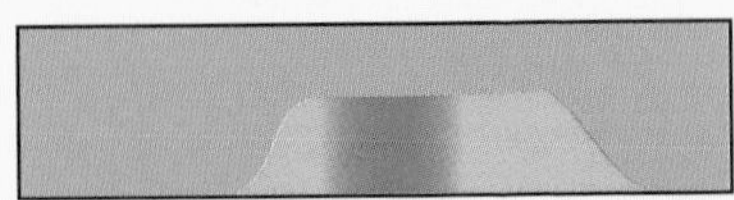

Yellow-rumped Warbler

Dendroica coronata

THIS SPIRITED SONGBIRD is as common as it is delightful. Its contrasting colours, curiosity, and tinkling trill are enthusiastically admired by even the most jaded birdwatcher.

The Yellow-rumped Warbler is the Cadillac of birds—it has all the extras. Although a few songbirds lack even a single distinguishing feature, this common Ontario warbler has them all. Wing bars, crown, breast streaks, coloured rump, light outer tail feathers, eyebrow, light throat and shoulder patches are just some of the extras to be found on this delightful model.

Quick ID: smaller than a sparrow; blue-black back, tail, and wings; yellow rump, shoulder patches, and crown; white throat; white wing bars; dark chest band; white belly; dark cheek; **Female:** less intense colours.

Size: 15 cm (6 in.)

Habitat: coniferous and mixed-wood forests, common in shrubs during migration.

Nest: often in conifers; cup of bark and plant material, on horizontal branch.

Food: insects, occasionally berries.

Foraging: gleans vegetation, flycatches and hovers.

Voice: faint trill that breaks and descends at the end.

Similar Species: Chestnut-sided Warbler (p. 114) and Canada Warbler lack combination of yellow rump and whitish underparts; Magnolia Warbler has a yellow throat and belly.

Notes: The species name *coronata* refers to this bird's bright yellow crown. • The eastern race of the Yellow-rumped Warbler was formerly called the Myrtle Warbler, while the western race (primarily restricted to British Columbia) was named the Audubon's Warbler in spite of the fact that it was one of the few birds the great ornithologist failed to meet.

Black-throated Green Warbler
Dendroica virens

HIGH UP IN TREE SPIRES lives the Black-throated Green Warbler. Conifer crowns are penthouses for neotropical warblers; many species choose to nest and forage exclusively at these great heights. If it weren't for the Black-throated Green's flitting habits and its unmistakable song, this warbler would often escape detection.

Because so many warbler species occur in the heights of our conifer forests, the food supply in these areas can come under pressure. Fortunately, many species of warbler can coexist because they partition the food supplies by foraging exclusively in certain areas. The Cape May Warbler holds rights to the very top of the tree, while Black-throated Greens feed just below, on the outer branches. These poorly understood interspecific relationships are doubtless vital to the stability of forest ecosystems.

Quick ID: smaller than a sparrow; yellow face; black throat; olive back; dark wings and tail; white wing bars; sexes similar; **Male:** has a larger black bib.

Size: 13 cm (5 in.)

Habitat: mature coniferous and mixed-wood forests.

Nest: small cup of fine plant materials; high in conifers.

Food: flying insects, caterpillars, other invertebrates.

Foraging: gleans vegetation, flycatches, hovers.

Voice: distinctive, high-pitched *see-see-see Su-zee.*

Similar Species: Black-throated Blue, Lawrence's, and Golden-winged Warblers all lack the black throat, green back and yellow face; Hooded Warbler has a black hood and overall yellow plumage.

Notes: There are a great many wood warblers that confine their breeding activities to mature forests. Agricultural and modern forestry methods that harvest trees on an 80- to 100-year rotation do not maintain the structural diversity of older forests; the growth of the younger forests is generally more uniform. Summer habitat loss is contributing to the decline of the Blackburnian, Cape May, Cerulean, Hooded, and other Warblers.

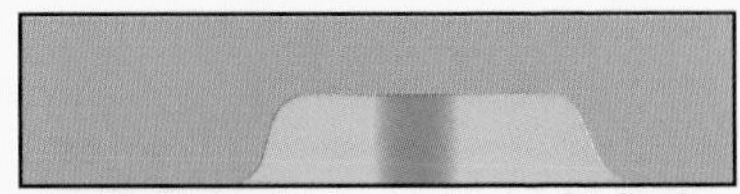

American Redstart
Setophaga ruticilla

LIKE AN OVER-ENERGIZED wind-up toy, the American Redstart flits from branch to branch in a dizzying pursuit of prey. Never for a moment will a Redstart pause, even while he's perched his orange-splashed tail waves gently.

This erratic and amusing behaviour is easily observed in the bird's summering ground as well as in its Central American wintering habitat, where it is affectionately known as *Candelita* ('the little candle'). With constantly quivering wings, tail, and shoulders, the Redstart's patches are sparks of life in any dark forest.

Since American Redstarts (and most other warblers) spend three-quarters of the year in Latin American forests and a scant three months in Canada, our often proprietary view of these species is not entirely justified.

Quick ID: smaller than a sparrow; **Male:** overall black with fiery orange patches in wings, tail, and shoulders; white belly; **Female:** olive-brown back; light underparts; peach-yellow patches in wings and tail and on shoulders.

Size: 13 cm (5 in.)

Habitat: deciduous and mixed-wood forests, shrubby understorey.

Nest: in shrubs; compact cup of grasses and fine plant materials, often in a tree fork.

Food: insects and other invertebrates.

Foraging: gleans vegetation, flycatches, hovers.

Jan Feb Mar Apr May Jun Jul Aug Sept Oct Nov Dec

Voice: variable, often a *tseet tseet see-o.*

Similar Species: there is no other predominantly black warbler; Red-winged Blackbird (p. 133) is much larger, with no red on chest and tail.

Notes: Ontario's Point Pelee National Park is internationally recognized as the premiere birding site for migrant wood warblers. Jutting out into Lake Erie, Pelee is the first point of land for birds flying north across that great lake in the spring. Exhausted warblers congregate on the peninsula to forage before continuing their northward migration. During mid-May, tens of thousands of birdwatchers flock to Pelee to experience the arrival of the warblers.

Ovenbird

Seiurus aurocapillus

THE OVENBIRD—or at least its song—is encountered frequently. Its loud and distinctive song announces its presence in deciduous woods, and its noisy habit of running through the undergrowth nearly reveals its precise location. This songbird's cryptic plumage and its stubborn habit of refusing to become airborne frustrate many birders intent on a quick peek. Rarely will Ovenbirds expose themselves to the open forest; they seem most comfortable in the tangle of shrubs, stumps and dead leaves.

The sharp, loud call of the Ovenbird rises from the dense layer of shrubs and plants and is one of the most distinctive voices of Ontario's forests.

Quick ID: sparrow-sized; heavily streaked breast; olive-brown back; russet crown bordered by black; orange legs; sexes similar.

Size: 16 cm (6 in.)

Habitat: mature deciduous or mixed-wood forests, little shrub cover.

Nest: on ground; globe made of grasses and fine plant material, shaped like a Dutch oven.

Food: insects, worms, spiders.

Foraging: gleans ground.

Voice: often repeated, fast, sharp *teacher-teacher-teacher* or perhaps more properly *pe-chur pe-chur pe-chur*, volume increases as song progresses.

Similar Species: Hermit (p. 101) and Wood Thrush (p. 102) are much larger, lack streaked russet crown; Northern Waterthrush lacks russet crown.

Notes: The Ovenbird's species name *aurocapillus* is Latin for 'golden hair,' an obvious reference to this bird's all too infrequently seen crown. • Henry David Thoreau (19th-century American naturalist and philosopher) was greatly frustrated in trying to learn the identity of what he called the 'Midnight Warbler,' a bird that sang wonderful melodies late at night. Although he often saw Ovenbirds in the vicinity of the 'Midnight Warbler' near his cabin on Walden Pond, Thoreau never imagined that his melodious mystery bird was actually the Ovenbird.

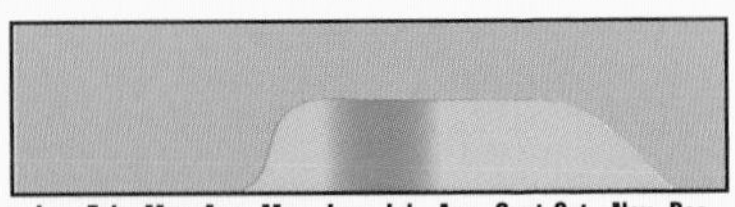

Jan Feb Mar Apr May Jun Jul Aug Sept Oct Nov Dec

Common Yellowthroat

Geothlypis trichas

THIS ENERGETIC WARBLER of the cattails is easily identified by its looks or by its sound. The male Common Yellowthroat's oscillating song is not easily forgotten. As this bird's name suggests, it is both common (it's one of the the most numerous warblers in North America) and yellow-throated. The male's characteristic black mask is an unmistakable field mark.

Female yellowthroats are rarely seen because they keep their nests deep within the thick vegetation surrounding marshes. Common Yellowthroats are a common host of cowbird eggs (see p. 136), but a stable and productive breeding population protects them from decline.

Quick ID: smaller than a sparrow; black mask and forehead; yellow underparts; olive back; orange legs; **Female:** lacks black mask.

Size: 13 cm (5 in.)

Habitat: cattail marshes, willows and alders, swamps and bogs.

Nest: in shrubs or cattails, on or near ground; loose cup of plant material.

Food: insects, other invertebrates.

Foraging: gleans vegetation, flycatches, occasionally hovers.

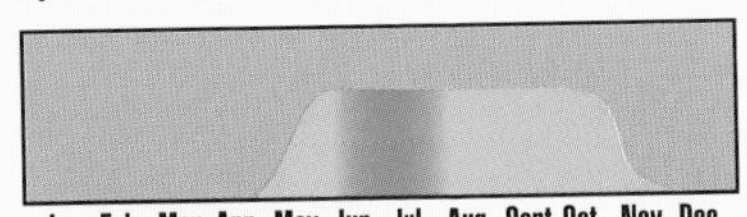

Voice: oscillating *witchety-witchety-witchety-witch*.

Similar Species: male distinct; female is similar to female Nashville Warbler (p. 112), but female Yellowthroat's legs are orange.

Notes: The call of the Common Yellowthroat is frequently heard in the company of Red-winged Blackbirds, Marsh Wrens, and Pied-billed Grebes. Sounds from various Ontario natural habitats are most distinctive, and a trained ear can determine landscape features such as wetlands, deciduous or coniferous forests by sound alone. The voices of birds are auditory trademarks of Ontario ecosystems.

Scarlet Tanager

Piranga olivacea

THE TROPICAL appearance of the Scarlet Tanager's plumage reinforces the link between the South American and Carolinian forests. A winter resident of the tropics and a breeder in Ontario mixed-woods, this tanager is vulnerable to deforestation at both extremes of its range.

Scarlet Tanagers can be difficult to see despite their tropical wardrobe as they tend to sing from high up in deciduous forest canopies. Because its song has the same quality as a robin's, the tanager is frequently disregarded as a common woodland voice. Novice bird-watchers should listen for its hiccup-like call as it cascades to the forest floor.

Quick ID: smaller than a robin; **Male:** unmistakable, magnificent scarlet body with contrasting black wings and tail; changes in the fall to look like female; **Female:** olive-yellow overall.

Size: 19 cm (7 in.)

Habitat: large deciduous and mixed-wood forests.

Nest: often in mature deciduous trees; shallow, loosely built nest, on horizontal branch far from trunk.

Food: insects, other invertebrates, berries.

Foraging: gleans vegetation, flycatches, hovers.

Voice: song: hoarse, robin-like warble: *hurry-worry-lurry-scurry*; call: *chick-burr*.

Similar Species: Northern Cardinal (p. 121); Baltimore Oriole (p. 137); Orchard Oriole; all lack combination of all-red body and black wings.

Notes: This bird's scientific name, *Piranga olivacea*, is Latin for 'olive tanager' and does not justly describe this splendid suitor. The original specimen collected and described had molted and lost its vivid colours. Unknowingly, the author described the bird as being olive, rather than the scarlet spectacle known to fortunate naturalists. • Ontarians are blessed with the spectacle of the Scarlet Tanager, but this is the only member of its 240-bird family that regularly breeds in Eastern Canada.

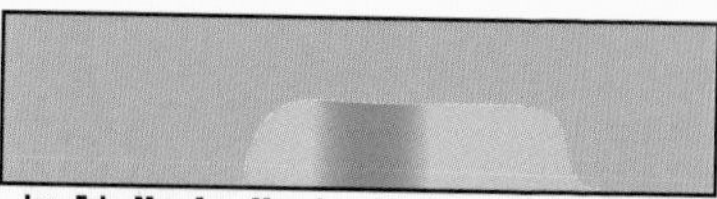

Northern Cardinal
Cardinalis cardinalis

THE GALLANTRY of the Northern Cardinal is not only found in its renowned attire—this pair's bond is one of the most faithful of Ontario's resident birds. Never far from one another, male and female Cardinals softly vocalize to one another during breeding season as if sharing sweet nothings. The ritualized beak-to-beak feeding reinforces the romantic appeal of these easily identifiable birds. Although the regal male does little more than warble to the female while she constructs the nest, his parental duties will soon keep him busy. After the eggs have hatched, the nestlings and the brooding female will remain in the nest while the male provides much of the food for the family.

This bird is becoming more common at backyard feeders, and many homeowners vividly remember the day their yards were first graced by Northern Cardinals. Hastily-taken colour photographs of these crimson birds jog memories of winter scenes.

Quick ID: smaller than a robin; **Male:** unmistakable; red overall; black mask and throat; pointed crest; red, conical bill; **Female:** similar to male except plumage quite a bit duller.

Size: 23 cm (9 in.)

Habitat: dense thickets, forest edges, city parks, brushy areas.

Nest: in tall, dense shrubs or small trees; loose bowl made of twigs and plant materials.

Food: invertebrates, berries, seeds, often sunflower seeds.

Jan Feb Mar Apr May Jun Jul Aug Sept Oct Nov Dec

Foraging: gleans ground.

Voice: quality is distinctive, phrases vary considerably: *What cheer! What cheer! Birdie-birdie-birdie what cheer!*

Similar Species: Scarlet Tanager (p. 120) has black wings and tail; Pine Grosbeak (p. 138) lacks a crest.

Notes: The settlement of Ontario has benefitted cardinals as they have immigrated up from the south. The first cardinal in Ontario was reported in 1849, and they have since established a strong foothold in the province. • This bird owes its name to Catholic cardinals, whose robes are a vivid red like the male of this species.

Rose-breasted Grosbeak

Pheucticus ludovicianus

MALE ROSE-BREASTED Grosbeaks have a voice that matches their magnificent plumage. Showing not the least concern for would-be predators, male Rose-breasted Grosbeaks flaunt their song and plumage in tree-top performances. This common songster's boldness does not go unnoticed by the appreciative birding community, which eagerly anticipates the male's annual spring concert. The male's outlandish plumage compensates for that of his unassuming mate, who lacks the formal dress but shares her partner's musical talents. Whether the nest is incubated by the male or female, the developing young are continually introduced into the world of song by the brooding parent.

Quick ID: smaller than a robin; **Male:** black hood; rose breast; black back and wings; white rump; white wing bars; light-coloured, conical bill; **Female:** heavily streaked with brown; white eyebrow; light-coloured, conical bill; light throat.

Size: 20 cm (8 in.)

Habitat: deciduous forests, often in ravines and along streams.

Nest: in shrub or tree; shallow bowl loosely made of twigs, grass, and vegetation.

Food: invertebrates, seeds, berries, buds.

Foraging: gleans vegetation, flycatches, hovers.

Voice: continuous, robin-like without pause, frequently sings bubbly *whip-poor-will* phrase.

Similar Species: male distinctive; female similar to female Purple Finch (p. 139) and to other sparrows, but generally larger.

Notes: Despite sharing a last name with the Evening and Pine Grosbeaks, the Rose-breasted Grosbeak shares no close phylogenetic relationship with them. • Bill characteristics are very 'plastic' in the evolutionary sense, meaning they change relatively quickly with time and conditions. As different families of birds have adapted to various food sources, similar traits (such as bill shape) are expressed within each group. • *Ludoviciana* is Latin meaning 'from Louisiana.'

Indigo Bunting

Passerina cyanea

METALLIC-BLUE male Indigo Buntings are frequently encountered along open areas of overgrown fields, and forest edges. Perched atop a shrub or thicket, the males conduct elaborate tactical manoeuvres with song. With rival males only a voice away, Indigo Buntings call continuously through the day to maintain superiority over their peers.

When the females arrive in Ontario, several days of vocal combat have already passed, and males have established their individual territorial boundaries. The female's interest lies in habitat and not song, but because the fittest males have generally established their territories within the finest habitat, the females end up choosing the most melodious mates.

Quick ID: sparrow-sized; **Male:** deep, iridescent blue overall; darker wings and tail; stubby, conical bill; **Female:** brown overall; light throat; stubby, conical bill.

Size: 14 cm (6 in.)

Habitat: edges of deciduous woodlands, brushy fields, hedgerows.

Nest: in low shrubs; well-made cup of woven grass, leaves, and other plant materials.

Food: invertebrates, seeds, berries.

Foraging: gleans vegetation and ground.

Voice: paired warbling couplets *fire-fire, where-where, here-here, see-it see-it.*

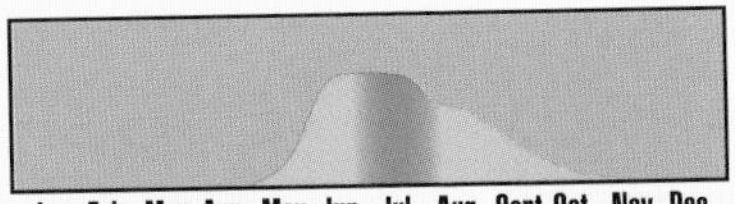

Similar Species: Eastern Bluebird (p. 99) has a red breast; female similar to many female sparrows, but is more mottled.

Notes: Birds are designed as flying machines and (with few exceptions) their body design is directly adapted to flight. To reduce weight, many of their bones are fused into smaller, stronger skeletal segments. Birds also lack teeth (which are heavy), and have much of their mass concentrated in the area between rump and head and not in extremities. In all other egg-laying animals (insects, fish, reptiles, etc.) there are always a few species that give birth to live young, but every living bird lays eggs. By having the young develop outside of the mother, female birds do not have to forsake flight during reproductive times.

Eastern Towhee
Pipilo erythrophthalmus

THIS LARGE, COCKY SPARROW is most often heard in the dense understorey before it is seen. The Eastern Towhee's characteristic double-scratching foraging technique rustles the dead leaves and grass beneath dense thickets. Squeaking and pishing is irresistible for towhees, who will quickly pop out from the cover to investigate the curious noise.

The male's black hood and back, white chest, and red flanks are characteristic of this species alone. With binoculars in bright light, you can also see this bird's blood-red eyes. The Eastern Towhee belts out a hearty *Drink your teeeea,* with an earnestness unsurpassed by any other bird. Until recently, this bird was known as the Rufous-sided Towhee.

Quick ID: smaller than a robin; black hood, back, and upper tail; rufous-coloured flanks; white tail underparts and outer tail feathers; red eyes; **Female:** reddish-brown rather than black on head and back.

Size: 22 cm (9 in.)

Habitat: woodland edges, shrubby areas, overgrown pastures.

Nest: bulky cup of grass, leaves and other vegetation; usually on ground, but sometimes low in shrub.

Food: terrestrial invertebrates, seeds, berries.

Foraging: gleans ground and vegetation.

Voice: clear, crisp *Drink your teeeea!*

Similar Species: American Robin (p. 103) is larger and lacks white on chest.

Notes: The art of pishing and squeaking is of great value for any aspiring naturalist. Although the act of producing the sound is quite easy, the nerve to pish and squeak (especially in public) often is lacking in novices. If you practise alone in the woods, you will not feel embarrassed or inadvertently shower a friend with an over-zealous pish. When you become comfortable with this new-found birding tool, you will be amazed at the diversity of life it will attract: birds, foxes, deer, cattle, birders, unknowing hikers....

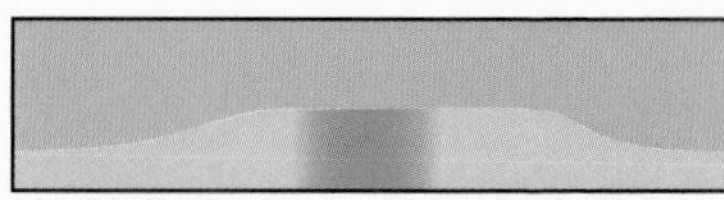

American Tree Sparrow

Spizella arborea

THE AMERICAN TREE SPARROW's annual flood into southern Ontario during late fall is a sign of the changing seasons. For the entire winter, these Arctic nesters decorate the leafless rural shrublands like ornaments on a Christmas tree. As one of the first songbirds to disappear in April and a regular arrival in late October, American Tree Sparrow activities quietly announce the closing of autumn and opening of spring.

These humble, quiet sparrows often go unnoticed despite their large numbers. American Tree Sparrows often visit city feeders during their migrations and while wintering in southern Ontario, but they never attempt to usurp the surly resident flock of House Sparrows and House Finches.

Quick ID: large sparrow; red crown; no white eyebrow; small central chest spot, breast otherwise unstreaked; back mottled; sexes similar.

Size: 16 cm (6 in.)

Habitat: breeds along treeline in extreme northern Ontario; overwinters in southern Ontario's forest edges, residential areas, fields.

Nest: small cup lined with feathers; usually on the ground or in short shrub, only in extreme northern Ontario (near treeline).

Food: invertebrates, seeds, buds, and catkins.

Foraging: gleans vegetation and ground.

Voice: generally quiet *tseet*.

Similar Species: Chipping Sparrow (p. 126); Field Sparrow; Swamp Sparrow; all lack faint breast spot.

Notes: While both its common and scientific name (*arborea* means 'tree') might imply that this sparrow prefers forests, that is not the case. As a bird that nests in the Arctic, where there is little more than shrubbery, the American Tree Sparrow is definitely not at home in tall trees. Although this subdued bird overwinters in good numbers in the United States, the only American soil on which it breeds is Alaska. With the hindsight of centuries of ornithological study, we may have chosen to designate this bird as the Arctic Shrub Sparrow, but we must forgive early ornithologists for the name slip-up, as they lacked the data that we have today.

Chipping Sparrow

Spizella passerina

HOPPING AROUND FRESHLY MOWED LAWNS, the cheery Chipping Sparrow goes about its business, unconcerned by the busy world that surrounds. Named for its call, the Chipping Sparrow is the most often seen red-capped sparrow in Ontario and is frequently encountered on lawns, in semi-open forests, and in mature forests.

Although it is very widely distributed, the Chipping Sparrow isn't the only red-capped sparrow in Ontario—there are many others. The Field Sparrow inhabits overgrown fields and young conifers; it lacks the characteristic black and white eyebrow of the Chipping Sparrow. As its name suggests, the Swamp Sparrow prefers wet areas of cattails and willow thickets, where it remains well hidden, cheating birdwatchers of a glimpse of its spritely grey face.

Quick ID: small sparrow; red crown; white eyebrow bordered by black; clean greyish breast; mottled back; sexes similar.

Size: 14 cm (6 in.)

Habitat: semi-open woodlands, suburban areas, parks, lawns.

Nest: neatly woven cup of grass and stalks; usually in conifers or shrubs.

Food: invertebrates, seeds.

Foraging: gleans ground and vegetation, flycatches.

Voice: call is a *chip, chip, chip, chip*; song is a fast trill.

Similar Species: American Tree Sparrow (p. 125, seen only in winter); Field Sparrow; Swamp Sparrow; all lack clean-lined white and black eyebrow.

Notes: So why *are* there so many darn sparrows and so few loon species? An easy answer would be that it's a curse put on would-be birders—all small brown birds tend to look alike, while large, resplendent waterbirds are most unique. But the real answer lies in the evolutionary process. Sparrows have relatively recently evolved and are still branching out and adapting to environmental change. Loons have been around a long time and have found a nice niche that suits them just fine.

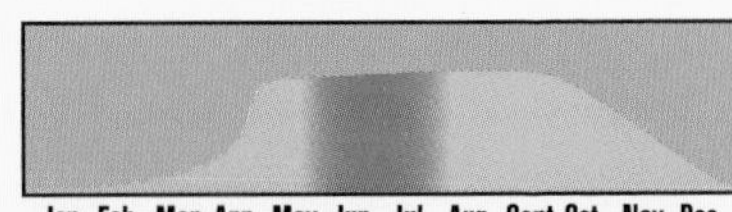

Savannah Sparrow

Passerculus sandwichensis

THIS BIRD'S DULL BROWN PLUMAGE and streaked breast conceal it perfectly in the long grasses of native prairie, farms and roadsides. It's most often seen darting across roads, highways, and open fields to escape intruders. Savannah Sparrows resort to flight only as a last alternative; they prefer to run swiftly and inconspicuously through the long grass, like feathered voles. The Savannah Sparrow's distinctive song and the yellow patch in front of each eye are the best ways to distinguish it from the many other grassland sparrows.

The Vesper Sparrow, which lives alongside the Savannah, is very similar to its neighbour; the Vesper is distinguished only by its chestnut shoulders and white outer tail feathers. The Vesper Sparrow concludes its song with a short musical trill, and it starts with four distinctive notes: *here here there there everybody down-the-hill.*

Quick ID: small sparrow; light chest streaking; mottled brown above; dark cheek; no white outer tail feathers; yellow lores; sexes similar.

Size: 14 cm (6 in.)

Habitat: grassy fields and grazed pastures.

Nest: small neat cups woven of grasses and plant fibres; on or very close to the ground.

Food: invertebrates, seeds.

Foraging: gleans ground.

Voice: buzzy trill dropping at the end: *Tea-tea-tea-teeea Today.*

Similar Species: Vesper Sparrow; Grasshopper Sparrow; Henslow's Sparrow; separated primarily by song.

Notes: The Savannah Sparrow is one of the most widespread species in North America. Open country in northern Ontario, along the coasts, in the Arctic, on remote islands, and in the bayous of the southern states, all host this common sparrow. In some areas where the breeding population is isolated from other Savannah Sparrows (such as on Sable Island in Nova Scotia, or on coastal California), distinct subspecies exist. Although these subspecies are locally known by different names (such as the Ipswich and Belding's Sparrows), they are not sufficiently different from the Savannah Sparrow (yet!) to be recognized as a distinct species.

Song Sparrow

Melospiza melodia

THE SONG SPARROW'S DRAB, heavily streaked plumage doesn't prepare you for its symphonic song. Although this common sparrow ends its tunes with a prolonged melody, it usually begins with three sharp *hip-hip-hip* notes. The tune conjures up ideas of far more exotic species than the sparrow family, which for the most part lacks the individual musical splendour of many finches and thrushes. Despite the bird's family roots, the song of the Song Sparrow stands among those of the great Ontario songsters in complexity and rhythm.

This summer breeder is encountered in a variety of habitats. The Song Sparrow is commonly heard in city parks, backyards, and mixed forests, and the effort that it expends delivering its song is commendable.

Quick ID: large sparrow; heavy breast streaks form central chest spot; plumage brown-red; striped head; white trailing down from bill; sexes similar.

Size: 16 cm (6 in.)

Habitat: throughout Ontario in shrubby habitats, often near water.

Nest: sturdy cup woven with plant fibres and grass; often on ground, occasionally in shrubs and tangles.

Food: invertebrates and seeds.

Foraging: gleans ground and vegetation.

Voice: series of warbles and buzzes, variable but resembling *Hip-hip-hip hooray boys, the spring is here again.*

Similar Species: Fox Sparrow has red stripes; Lincoln's and Vesper Sparrows have weaker breast streaks.

Notes: Song Sparrows (and many other songbirds) learn to sing by eavesdropping on their fathers or on rival males. This influence is so great that by the time the male is a few months old, he will have the basis for his song. Some studies have shown that certain songbirds that are exposed to foreign songs through their development retain and repeat the foreign songs rather than their natural tunes.

Jan Feb Mar Apr May Jun Jul Aug Sept Oct Nov Dec

White-throated Sparrow

Zonotrichia albicollis

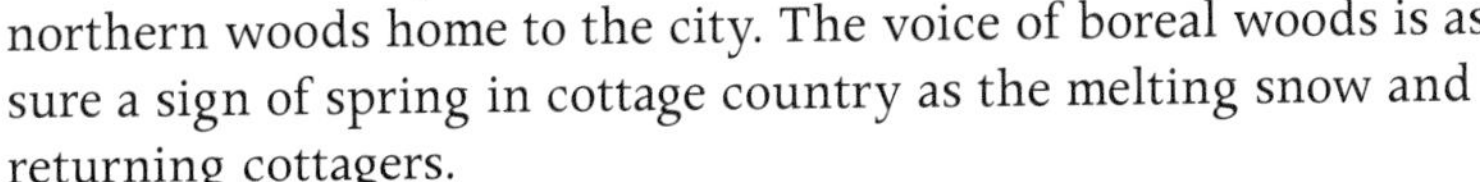

THE CATCHY SONG of the White-throated Sparrow is often on the lips of weekend cottagers returning from the country. By whistling the distinctive *Dear sweet Canada-Canada-Canada* to themselves, people bring some of the atmosphere of the northern woods home to the city. The voice of boreal woods is as sure a sign of spring in cottage country as the melting snow and returning cottagers.

In winter, a few White-throated Sparrows migrate into town, where birdfeeders provide them with a steady supply of seed without much physical exertion. Its striped head and white throat allow this forest breeder to stand out from other sparrows and from House Finches.

Quick ID: large sparrow; black and white striped head; white throat; unstreaked, light grey breast; yellow lores; rusty-brown upperparts; tan phase has brownish, rather than white, streaks on head; sexes similar.

Size: 17 cm (7 in.)

Habitat: large, semi-open mixed-wood and conifer forests.

Nest: sturdy cup woven with grasses, twigs, and wood chips; usually on the ground or very low in a shrub.

Food: invertebrates, seeds, berries.

Foraging: gleans ground, flycatches.

Voice: *Dear sweet Canada-Canada-Canada*, often sung at night.

Similar Species: White-crowned Sparrow lacks white throat.

Notes: The next time you make a summertime visit to Algonquin Park or cottage country, time how long it takes until you hear the first White-throated Sparrow—it won't be long. • Song paraphrases are often very individualistic—what works for you may not help others. The White-throat's call is frequently paraphrased as *Old Sam Peabody Peabody Peabody* in the United States, where many of these birds overwinter. • *Zonotrichia* means 'hair-like,' referring to this bird's striped head, and *albicollis* is Latin for 'white neck.'

Dark-eyed Junco

Junco hyemalis

JUNCOS ARE GROUND DWELLERS, and are frequently observed flushing along wooded trails. The distinctive white outer tail feathers will flash in alarm as the otherwise dark junco flies down the narrow path before diving into a thicket. From thickets and trees, Dark-eyed Juncos sing their descending trills, which sound very much like those of the Chipping Sparrow. The confusion can build as both the Junco and the Sparrow occur in similar habitats, so a confirmation of identity usually requires a visual search. The Dark-eyed Junco does occasionally identify itself by sound, but not by its confusing song. The junco's distinctive smacking call, and the bird's habit of double-scratching at forest litter, effectively betray its identity. Dark-eyed Juncos are common winter visitors in southern Ontario, and they are frequent guests at bird feeders, usually picking up the scraps that have fallen to the ground.

Quick ID: large sparrow; slate-grey; light-coloured bill; white outer tail feathers; white belly; sexes similar.

Size: 16 cm (6 in.)

Habitat: breeds in central and northern Ontario conifer and mixed-wood forests; overwinters along southern Ontario forest edges and in residential areas.

Nest: sturdy cup of grasses and plant fibres; usually on the ground in depressions or in hollow logs.

Food: seeds, invertebrates, birdfeeder seeds.

Foraging: gleans ground, flycatches.

Voice: simple trill (very similar to that of a Chipping Sparrow); also a smacking call note.

Similar Species: Bobolink (p. 132); Brown-headed Cowbird (p. 136); both lack white outer tail feathers.

Notes: Seed-eating birds such as juncos tend to have stout, conical bills. The shape of the bill enables the bird to use maximum force to crack seeds. Although seed cracking may appear to be a hurried affair, a seed-eating bird uses its tongue to carefully place the seed in the most powerful part of its bill before cracking down.

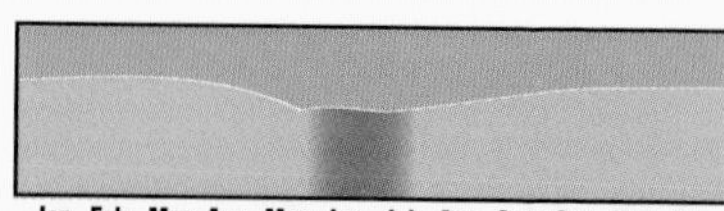

Snow Bunting
Plectrophenax nivalis

ONCE THE BREEDING SONGBIRDS have gone and the first winter storm has blanketed southern Ontario, Snow Buntings arrive from the Arctic and settle in for winter. Thousands can congregate in windswept fields; they scratch at the frozen soil to uncover grain left over from autumn.

During winter, Snow Buntings are rarely seen alone. Their large flocks are accustomed to the ground, because Snow Buntings spend all of their lives in areas where there are few places to perch. On a cold winter day, it is a special treat to watch a flock of Snow Buntings, occasionally numbering in the thousands, rise up in unison. The way they move with their black and white plumage gives the illusion that the flock is appearing and disappearing against the snowy backdrop.

Quick ID: sparrow-sized; black wingtips on white wings (distinctive in flight); black tail with white streaks; cinnamon back and crown; snow-white belly; sexes similar.

Size: 17 cm (7 in.)

Habitat: breeds above treeline in Ontario and elsewhere; overwinters in southern Ontario fields and agricultural lands.

Nest: bulky bowl of grass, lichens, and plant fibres; usually on the ground or on a cliff.

Food: plant seed, waste grain, insects during summer.

Foraging: gleans ground.

Voice: song is a musical, high-pitched *chi-chi-churee* (heard only on breeding grounds); call is a whistled *tew.*

Similar Species: Lapland Longspur is less common and lacks bold black and white plumage.

Notes: *Plectrophenax* is Greek for 'an impostor that lacks a hind claw,' while *nivalis* is Latin for 'snow.' Open-country sparrows and buntings often have a very long hind claw, which is an adaptation to their terrestrial and not arboreal lifestyle. The Snow Bunting lacks this long spur (hence 'impostor') but does have relatively longer leg bones to suit its terrestrial habits. • The breeding colours of the Snow Bunting are an example of contrast: jet black wings and tail, snowy white body plumage. Unfortunately, most Buntings have left southern Ontario before they acquire their splendid dress.

Bobolink

Dolichonyx oryzivorus

DURING THE SPRING, small flocks of Bobolinks return to hayfields in southern Ontario to grace the cool mornings with their songs. The male Bobolink, with its dark belly and light upperparts, is coloured like no other bird in Ontario; the female is dressed in sparrow drabs. Although Bobolinks look and live like large sparrows, their polygynous breeding strategy hints at their blackbird roots. A colourful and vociferous male that acquires a prime hayfield may mate with and defend several females.

The fall migration of Bobolinks is one of the largest and longest of the songbirds. Flocks numbering in the thousands congregate through the U.S. to travel to South American pastures. Along their southern journey, large Bobolink flocks were once dreaded as the 'Rice Birds' that stuffed themselves upon the ripening crops. Because of their destructive habits Bobolinks were once so effectively controlled that their present population has yet to recover.

Quick ID: sparrow-sized; **Breeding Male:** mostly black; buffy nape; white rump and wing patches; non-breeding plumage similar to female; **Female:** dull brown overall; streaking on back and flanks; brown stripes on head.

Size: 18 cm (7 in.)

Habitat: hayfields, meadows.

Nest: shallow cup woven with grass and plant fibres; on the ground.

Food: invertebrates, plant seeds.

Foraging: gleans ground and vegetation.

Voice: bubbling, banjo-like twangs: *bob-o-link bob-o-link, spink, spank, spink.*

Similar Species: Dark-eyed Junco (p. 130); Brown-headed Cowbird (p. 136); both have dark backs.

Notes: Like the Bobolink, quite a few birds derive their name from their songs or calls: the Killdeer, Sora, Eastern Phoebe, Eastern Wood-Pewee, Northern Bobwhite, Willet, Common Poorwill, Whip-poor-will, Chuck-will's Widow, and Dickcissel are some of them. • The paraphrase of the Bobolink's song used above is from the poem 'Robert of Lincoln,' by American poet William Cullen Bryant.

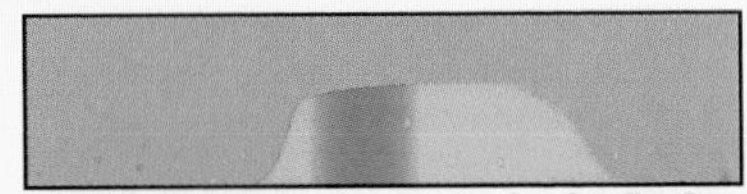

Jan Feb Mar Apr May Jun Jul Aug Sept Oct Nov Dec

Red-winged Blackbird

Agelaius phoeniceus

NO CATTAIL MARSH is free from the loud calls and bossy, aggressive nature of the Red-winged Blackbird. The male's bright red shoulders are his most important tool in the often strategic and intricate displays he uses to defend his territory from rivals. In experiments, males whose red shoulders were painted black soon lost their territories to rivals that they had previously defeated.

The female's interest lies not in the individual combatants, but in nesting habitat, and a male who can successfully defend a large area of dense cattails will breed with many females. After the females have built their concealed nests and laid their eggs, the male continues his persistent vigil, accosting and intimidating potential predators and unwary vagrants.

Quick ID: smaller than a robin; **Male:** all-black plumage with red and yellow shoulder patch (yellow not always evident); **Female:** brown overall; heavily streaked; only a hint of red on shoulder.

Size: 22 cm (9 in.)

Habitat: wetland marshes, willows.

Nest: bulky bowl woven of grass, plant fibres, cattail shreds, and leaves; low in cattails or other non-woody plants.

Food: invertebrates, seeds.

Foraging: gleans ground and vegetation, flycatches.

Voice: raspy, loud *konk-a-reee* or *eat my CHEEEzies*.

Similar Species: Rusty Blackbird; Common Grackle (p. 135); both lack red shoulder patches.

Notes: Male Red-winged Blackbirds arrive at the marshes and wetlands of Ontario a week or so before the females. In the ladies' absence, the males stake out territories through song and visual displays. A flashy and richly voiced male who has managed to establish a large and productive territory may attract several mates to his cattail mansion. • While wintering in Texas, Red-winged Blackbirds flock together with other blackbirds, forming swarms of tens of thousands of birds that can cause much damage to grain crops.

Eastern Meadowlark

Sturnella magna

EASTERN MEADOWLARKS are well adapted to the landscape of the fields and pastures where they spend their summers. In the East, the song of the meadowlark is a signature of open areas. Eastern Meadowlarks are both showy and perfectly camouflaged. Their yellow chest, with its black 'V,' and their white outer tail feathers serve to attract mates—and predators. Potential meadowlark mates face one another, raise their bills high and perform a grassland ballet. Oddly, the colourful breast and white tail feathers are also used to attract the attention of potential predators and mates. As foxes, hawks, or falcons focus on these bold features in pursuit, their prey mysteriously disappears into the grass whenever the meadowlark chooses to turn its back or fold away its white tail flags.

Quick ID: robin-sized; mottled brown upperparts; black 'V' on chest; yellow throat and belly; white outer tail feathers; striped head; sexes similar.

Size: 24 cm (10 in.)

Habitat: uncultivated fields, grazed pastures.

Nest: domed nest, woven with grass and plant fibres; always on the ground among grass clumps.

Food: invertebrates, seeds.

Foraging: gleans ground.

Voice: flute-like melody: *This is the Year* or *Spring of the Year*.

Similar Species: Western Meadowlark has more yellow on its cheek and a different song.

Notes: Western Meadowlarks also occur in southern Ontario but are certainly more scarce. The western version of these great singers is so similar to the eastern that they are virtually indistinguishable except for their voices. Although this small fact may arouse concern in novice bird-watchers, meadowlarks are continuous singers, so identification is not long in coming. The Western Meadowlark's distinctive song is the voice of the Canadian prairies.

Jan Feb Mar Apr May Jun Jul Aug Sept Oct Nov Dec

Common Grackle

Quiscalus quiscula

THE COMMON GRACKLE is a noisy and cocky bird that prefers to feed on the ground in open areas. Bird feeders in rural areas can attract large numbers of these blackish birds, whose cranky disposition drives away most other birds (even the quarrelsome Blue Jays and House Sparrows). The Common Grackle is easily identified by its long tail, large bill, and dark plumage, which may shine with hues of green, purple, and blue in bright light.

The Common Grackle is a poor but spirited singer. Usually while perched in a shrub, a male grackle will slowly take a deep breath that inflates his chest and causes his feathers to rise. Then he closes his eyes and gives out a loud, surprising *swaaaack*. Despite our perception of the Common Grackle's musical weakness, following his 'song' the male smugly and proudly poses with his bill held high.

Quick ID: Blue Jay-sized; glossy black; plumage faintly iridescent; long tail; large bill; sexes similar.

Size: 32 cm (13 in.)

Habitat: variable; marshes, young forests, agricultural areas.

Nest: bulky bowl woven with grass, sticks, plant fibres, leaves; always in shrubs or trees.

Food: diverse; terrestrial and aquatic invertebrates, seeds, small vertebrates, other birds' eggs.

Foraging: gleans ground and vegetation.

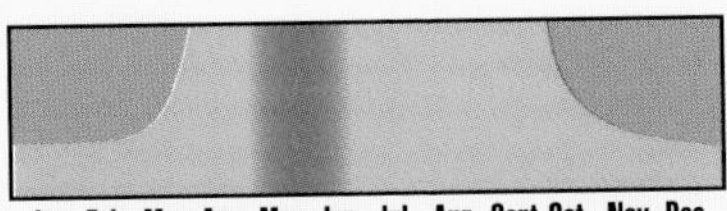

Voice: quick, loud *swaaaack*.

Similar Species: Rusty Blackbird; Brewer's Blackbird; Brown-headed Cowbird (p. 136); American Crow (p. 90); all have relatively shorter tails.

Notes: *Quiscalus* is New Latin meaning 'quail,' which is odd since the Common Grackle is clearly not at all similar to those frisky game birds, except perhaps in flight behaviour. • While the Common Grackle is fairly distinct in southern Ontario, in central and northern Ontario it may be confused with the Rusty and Brewer's Blackbirds. Both these glossy relatives of the grackle lack its long tail and heavy bill, and they spend much less time on the ground than does the cocky grackle.

Brown-headed Cowbird
Molothrus ater

THIS SMALL BLACK BIRD with a chocolate-brown head is quickly becoming one of the most hated native birds in North America. Brown-headed Cowbirds eat grain, but they're not considered an agricultural pest—it is their treatment of other songbirds that frustrates many bird enthusiasts.

Historically, Brown-headed Cowbirds followed the bison, so these vagabonds were constantly on the move and were unable to tend a nest. To overcome this problem, cowbirds laid their eggs in the nests of other songbirds, which, not recognizing the difference, raised the young cowbirds as their own. Unfortunately for the unwilling host, the young cowbirds are very aggressive; they will win out over the foster parent's own offspring, which often die from lack of food. Cowbirds now follow ranch mammals, and the expansion of ranching and the fragmentation of forests have significantly increased the cowbird's range.

Quick ID: larger than a sparrow
Male: metallic glossy black plumage; soft brown head; dark eye;
Female: brownish-grey overall; dark eye; slight chest streaks.

Size: 19 cm (8 in.)

Habitat: grassy areas, agricultural fields, forest edges.

Nest: none-brood parasite; most common hosts are small songbirds such as the Chipping Sparrow, Yellow Warbler, Song Sparrow, and Red-eyed Vireo.

Food: invertebrates, seeds.

Foraging: gleans ground.

Voice: squeaky, high-pitched; call: *weee-tse-tse*; song: *glug-glug-gu-leee*.

Similar Species: Rusty Blackbird; Brewer's Blackbird; Common Grackle (p. 135); all have body plumage similar to their head colour.

Notes: As the rapidly growing cowbird develops, it soon becomes larger than the rightful nestlings and often outsizes its foster parent. It is an emotional sight to witness a parasitized warbler feeding a begging cowbird while its own offspring slowly starve. Despite these individual tragedies, many species have adapted to the cowbird's parasitism (e.g., by building a new nest over the old, ejecting the foreign egg, or abandoning the nest altogether), and only those species of the forest's interior are truly threatened by encroaching cowbirds.

Baltimore Oriole
Icterus galbula

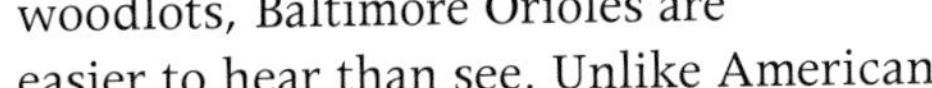

ALTHOUGH THEY are common residents of city parks and woodlots, Baltimore Orioles are easier to hear than see. Unlike American Robins, which inhabit the human domain of shrubs and lawns, Baltimore Orioles nest and feed in the tallest deciduous trees available. Their hanging, pouch-like nests, which are deceptively strong, are easily seen after the leaves have fallen in autumn, and a vacant nest is often the only confirmation that a pair of orioles summered in an area.

The male oriole's striking black and orange plumage complements his robin-like song. The slow and purposeful *Peter Peter here here Peter Peter* is repeated in early spring from atop tall trees. With only a little effort, many neighbourhood songs previously attributed to robins will, upon investigation, reveal a beautiful Baltimore Oriole.

Quick ID: robin-sized; **Male:** brilliant orange belly flanks and rump; black hood, wings, and tail; **Female:** like a washed-out male; faint hood.

Size: 22 cm (9 in.)

Habitat: mature deciduous forests, city parks.

Nest: suspended woven pouch of grass, plant fibres, fur, and synthetic fibres, always high in a deciduous tree.

Food: invertebrates, berries, nectar.

Foraging: gleans vegetation, flycatches.

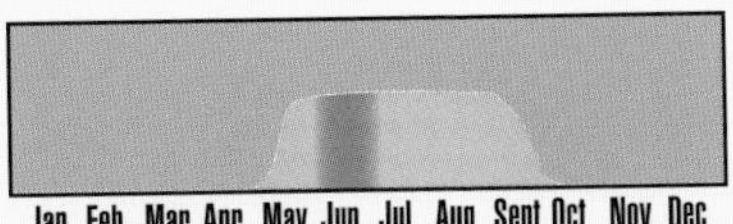

Voice: slow, flowing warble: *Peter Peter here here Peter Peter.*

Similar Species: Orchard Oriole breeds only in southwestern Ontario, males are chestnut where the Baltimore Oriole is orange, female is yellow-green.

Notes: The genus name *Icterus* is Greek for 'jaundice,' and *galbula* is New Latin for 'small yellow bird.' An old custom used to cure a person of jaundice was to show them a yellowish-green bird. Apparently the person was somehow mysteriously cured, but unfortunately the bird died. Although the scientific credibility of this remedy is questionable at best, there is little doubt of the soothing effects that a breeding male oriole has on the spirit.

Pine Grosbeak
Pinicola enucleator

A SPECIES OF THE GREAT BOREAL FOREST, the Pine Grosbeak is a bird common to northern areas alone. Zealous American birders have travelled great distances just to see one of Ontario's famed winter finches. Although it is not extremely common in southern Ontario, this hardy bird will almost certainly be seen on a winter trip to cottage country. When out searching for this noteworthy finch, search the tops of spruce and pine; the spires are favourite perching sites for the Grosbeak. The prize when out 'pining' for Grosbeaks is the sight of a mature male. Its splendid red plumage strikes a vivid contrast against the snow and spruce bows upon which it frequently perches.

Quick ID: robin-sized; **Males:** rich red body; black wings and tail; large (*gros*), slightly hooked bill; white wing bars; stocky; **Females and Immatures:** grey-olive body plumage, otherwise similar.

Size: 25 cm (10 in.)

Habitat: breeds in northern coniferous woods; overwinters (in some years) in southern Ontario forests, residential areas (irruptive).

Nest: bulky cup of grasses, twigs, lichens; usually high in a conifer.

Food: seeds of conifers and hardwoods, berries, insects, sunflower seeds.

Foraging: gleans vegetation and ground.

Voice: short musical warble.

Similar Species: Purple Finch (p. 139); House Finch (p. 140); Red Crossbill; White-winged Crossbill (p. 141); all are smaller and lack large, black beak; female Evening Grosbeak (p. 145) has a larger white wing patch.

Notes: *Pinicola* is Latin for 'a pine dweller,' and *enucleator* is Latin for 'one who deshells.' As a bird that frequently forages on seeds and fruit, its name and its powerful bill are very suitable. • Fortunate residents with winter feeders are blessed with the colours and activities of both the Pine and Evening Grosbeaks. With such a sight to experience daily, winters must surely pass with much less monotony.

Purple Finch
Carpodacus purpureus

THE PURPLE FINCH breeds throughout central Ontario and sporadically in southern Ontario, but outside of the breeding season it is most often seen at winter feeders. Purple Finches are a blessing to see on cold winter days; their raspberry plumage differs slightly from that of the more common House Finches. Although their numbers vary from year to year and they can be common in certain neighbourhoods, Purple Finches are never discounted as a standard backyard bird. When backyard bird enthusiasts list the birds visiting their winter feeders, the Purple Finch is usually mentioned along with Cardinals and Blue Jays.

Quick ID: sparrow-sized; forked tail; **Male:** raspberry head, nape, throat, and rump; reddish-brown cheek; streaked back; white undertail coverts; **Female:** brown overall; underparts streaked; white eyebrow; brown cheek.

Size: 15 cm (6 in.)

Habitat: breeds in central and northern Ontario coniferous and mixed-wood forests; overwinters in central and southern Ontario in rural and residential areas.

Nest: shallow cup woven with grass, spruce twigs, and plant fibres; usually in conifers.

Food: plant seed, invertebrates, berries, birdfeeder seed.

Foraging: gleans ground and vegetation.

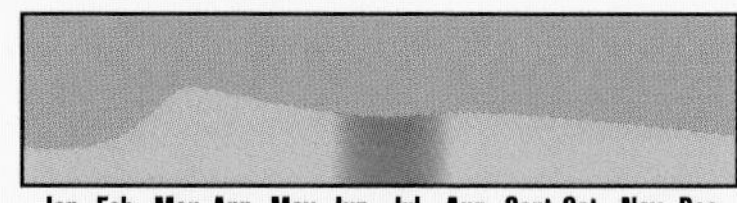

Voice: bubbly warble.

Similar Species: male House Finch (p. 140) has brown streaks on underparts, female House Finch lacks distinct brown cheek patch; female Rose-breasted Grosbeak (p. 122) is larger than female finch and has white wing bars.

Notes: When jotting down field notes it is often difficult to write down the entire name of a bird because of time constraints. For this reason, ornithologists have developed an effective and simple-to-use rule to abbreviate the names of birds. The four-letter codes usually use the first two letters of the species' first and last common name (e.g., Purple Finch = PUFI). It is slightly more complicated when the bird has only a one-word name (e.g., Bobolink = BOBO) or when it has three or more words (Red-winged Blackbird = RWBL, or Black-throated Green Warbler = BTGW).

House Finch
Carpodacus mexicanus

THE MALE'S RED FRONT END easily distinguishes the common House Finch from most other streaky brown backyard feeder birds. During the 1920s and 1930s, these birds, native to the American Southwest, were popular cage birds, sold across the continent as Hollywood Finches. Illegal releases of the caged birds, and expansion from their historic range, have resulted in two separate distributions in North America that are destined to converge. Ontario's House Finches are the descendants of cage birds released in New York in the 1940s. In three short decades, the New York birds invaded Ontario, and were first recorded breeding here in 1978.

As the House Finch continues to expand its range, becoming one of the most common birds in North America, it symbolizes both the intentional and the indirect results of human intervention on wildlife communities.

Quick ID: sparrow-sized; squared tail; **Male:** deep red forehead, eyebrow, and throat; buffy grey belly; brown cheek; streaked undertail coverts; **Female:** brown overall; streaked underparts; lacks eyebrow.

Size: 15 cm (6 in.)

Habitat: residential areas, farmyards.

Nest: small cup woven with grass, twigs, and plant fibres; usually in conifers.

Food: plant seed, berries, birdfeeder seed, very few invertebrates.

Foraging: gleans ground and vegetation.

Voice: warble lasting 3 seconds, last note ascends.

Similar Species: Purple Finch (p. 139) is less red and has pure white undertail coverts, female Purple Finch has brown cheek.

Notes: Although House Finches are generally confined to residential and urban areas, they continue to radiate out into surrounding communities. Most large cities in southern Ontario currently hold strong populations, and House Finches are continually moving to the north and west. If your backyard feeder continues to remain free of House Finches, be patient—they're on their way.

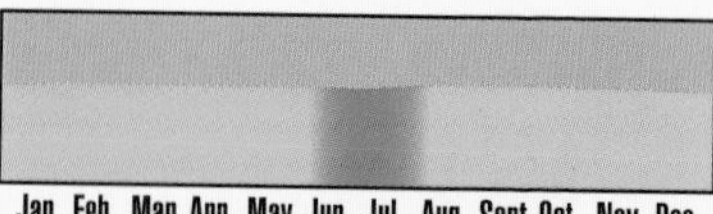

White-winged Crossbill
Loxia leucoptera

NOVICE BIRDERS FREQUENTLY MEASURE how exotic a bird is by its bill size and shape. The bills of tropical toucans, hornbills, and cassowaries are elaborate, but the boreal forests of Ontario also host a bird with a most particular bill. The tips of the crossbill's beak overlap, leaving the bird with a seemingly clumsy foraging instrument, but crossbills primarily eat spruce seeds and their bills are perfectly designed to pry open the cones. The crossbill pries open the cone scales by closing its bill (allowing the bill tips to separate the overlapping scales) and seizing the sought-after seed with its tongue. Because crossbills overwinter in flocks, a foraging group high in a spruce tree creates an unforgettable shower of spruce cone scales and crackling chatter.

Quick ID: sparrow-sized; **Male:** dark pink body; black wings and tail; broad, white wing bars; **Female:** greenish-yellow body.

Size: 17 cm (6 in.)

Habitat: breeds in mature coniferous forests in central and northern Ontario; overwinters in southern Ontario conifers (very sporadically).

Nest: cup woven of twigs, moss and grass; always in mature conifers.

Food: conifer seeds, also some insects and berries.

Foraging: gleans vegetation.

Voice: high-pitched series of trills.

Similar Species: Red Crossbill lacks white wing bars and is deeper red; Pine Grosbeak (p. 138) has a much larger, conical bill; Pine Siskin (p. 143) has a yellow tail and white wing lining.

Notes: *Loxia* is Greek for 'cross-wise,' *leucopetera* means 'white wing.' • When not foraging high in spruce spires, White-winged Crossbills are frequently seen licking salt from winter roads. • Red Crossbills can also be common during some winters, but they prefer pine trees over spruce. • By observing conifers in late fall, an attentive naturalist can predict with some accuracy whether crossbills will appear during the winter. White-winged Crossbill irruptions often coincide with heavy crops of spruce cones, their primary food.

Common Redpoll

Carduelis flammea

COMMON BUT UNPREDICTABLE winter visitors to southern Ontario, redpolls can frequently be seen snowplowing through soft powder. Wintering redpolls can forage atop the snow, picking fallen seeds from its surface, or plucking at emergent grass heads. The redpoll does not wade deep into the snow; its fluffy body allows this tiny bird to float on the softest snow without sinking beyond its belly.

When great flocks of Common Redpolls descend into birch trees along forest edges or to feeders in southern Ontario, scan the flocks carefully for unusual plumages. Mixed in with large flocks of Common Redpolls is often a lightly coloured redpoll with an unstreaked rump; this bird is known as the Hoary Redpoll. Hoary Redpolls are actually considered a true and valid species in their own right, but their distinction may be better attributed to species-starved winter bird-watchers, rather than to flawless scientific scrutiny.

Quick ID: sparrow-sized; heavy brown streaks on light body; red forehead; black chin; **Male:** has a rosy breast.

Size: 13 cm (5 in.)

Habitat: breeds (in Ontario) at or above treeline along coast of Hudson Bay; overwinters in southern Ontario forest edges.

Nest: in extreme northern Ontario, in Arctic willows; sturdy cup woven with twigs and plant fibres.

Food: seeds of shrubs and birch trees, birdfeeder seed, insects in summer.

Foraging: gleans ground and vegetation.

Voice: song: twittering and trills; call: soft *chit-chit-chit-chit*, also *swe-eet.*

Similar Species: Hoary Redpoll is light-coloured; Pine Siskin (p. 143); sparrows; all lack red forehead and black chin.

Notes: Winter finches (and other winter birds) are very well insulated from the cold. The degree of insulation can be seen in a very simple experiment. If you find a dead and frozen bird during the winter, take it inside to see how long it takes to thaw. Surprisingly, some species require several days at room temperature before all the frost is released.

Pine Siskin
Carduelis pinus

TIGHT FLOCKS OF THESE GREGARIOUS BIRDS are frequently heard before they are seen. Their characteristic call starts off slowly and then climbs to a high-pitched climax. Once you recognize this distinctive call, a flurry of activity in the tree tops, showing occasional flashes of yellow, will confirm the presence of Pine Siskins.

Like most other winter finches, the heavily streaked siskin is subject to periodic population irruptions into southern Ontario. When conditions for siskins breeding in northern and central Ontario do not promote overwintering, these small birds flood into the southern areas, where they readily find food in fields and forests, and in backyard feeders.

Quick ID: sparrow-sized; heavily streaked; yellow flashes in wings and tail; dull brown plumage; sexes similar.

Size: 13 cm (5 in.)

Habitat: breeds in central and northern Ontario mixed and conifer woodlands; overwinters sporadically along forest edges in southern Ontario.

Nest: shallow cup woven with conifer twigs, bark, and plant down; usually in a conifer.

Food: plant seed, invertebrates.

Foraging: gleans vegetation and ground.

Voice: song: goldfinch-like but more coarse and bubbling; call: prolonged, accelerating and rising *zweeeeeet*.

Similar Species: Song Sparrow (p. 128); female finches; female crossbills; all lack yellow wing and tail linings.

Notes: Most winter finches are irruptive to a certain degree, and the conditions (food, cold, snow cover) prompting their outbursts are not well understood. Many irruptions appear to be cyclical, but that is not always the case. Classic irruptive species in Ontario are Bohemian Waxwing, Pine Grosbeak, Evening Grosbeak, Hoary Redpoll, Common Redpoll, White-winged Crossbill, Red Crossbill, Purple Finch, and Pine Siskin.

American Goldfinch

Carduelis tristis

THE AMERICAN GOLDFINCH is a bright, cheery songbird that is commonly seen in weedy fields, roadsides and backyards, where it often feeds on thistle seeds. The American Goldfinch delays nesting until June to ensure a dependable source of thistles and dandelion seeds to feed its young.

The American Goldfinch is absent from much of northern Ontario during winter, but for those that do not choose a Mexican or American retreat, southern Ontario feeders seem quite adequate. When the great southern flocks return in late spring, and the overwintering birds regain their courting spirit, American Goldfinches swing over fields in their distinctive, undulating flight, and fill the air with their jubilant voices.

Quick ID: sparrow-sized; **Breeding Male:** black forehead, wings, and tail; canary-yellow body; wings show white in flight; **Female and Winter Male:** lack black forehead; yellow-green overall; black wings and tail.

Size: 13 cm (5 in.)

Habitat: weedy fields, overgrown pastures, and forest edges.

Nest: compact cups woven with grass, plant down, and plant fibres; usually in low shrubs.

Food: thistle seeds, other seeds, a few invertebrates, birdfeeder seed.

Foraging: gleans vegetation and ground.

Voice: song: *po-ta-to-chip*, often delivered in flight; call: *dear-me, see-me?*

Similar Species: Evening Grosbeak (p. 145) is much larger; Yellow Warbler (p. 113) has no black on forehead or wings.

Notes: Because goldfinches are commonly bullied at feeders by House Finches and House Sparrows, the great birdfeeder inventor minds have recently made a feeder for goldfinches alone. The acrobatic American Goldfinches will not hesitate to feed while hanging upside down, whereas the bold bullies refuse to invert for seed. Cylinder feeders designed just for goldfinches therefore have the seed opening positioned below the perches. It is most entertaining to watch goldfinches flip for seed, while frustrated House Sparrows search in vain for an opening.

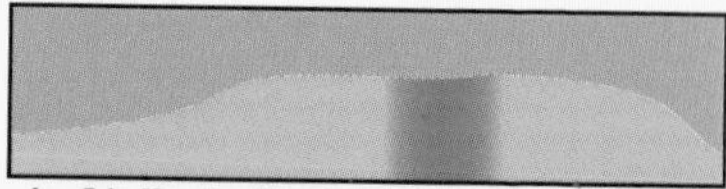

Evening Grosbeak
Coccothraustes vespertinus

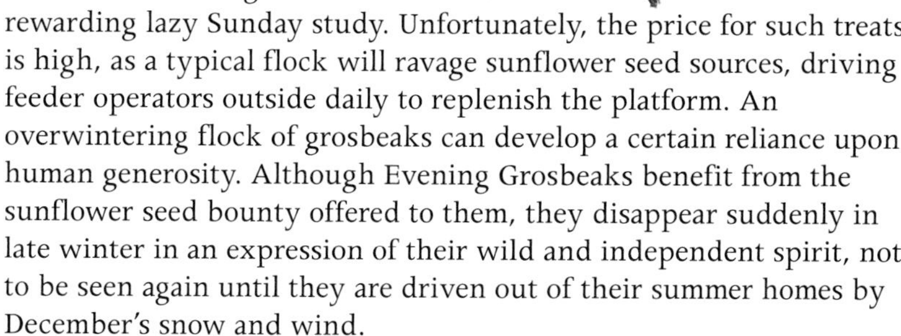

UNANNOUNCED, a flock of Evening Grosbeaks descends one chilly December day upon a feeder. For the proprietor of the feeder, the gold and black grosbeaks are both a blessing and a curse. The males' colour is unmatched by other winter bird attire, and the complex social interaction of a large flock makes for a rewarding lazy Sunday study. Unfortunately, the price for such treats is high, as a typical flock will ravage sunflower seed sources, driving feeder operators outside daily to replenish the platform. An overwintering flock of grosbeaks can develop a certain reliance upon human generosity. Although Evening Grosbeaks benefit from the sunflower seed bounty offered to them, they disappear suddenly in late winter in an expression of their wild and independent spirit, not to be seen again until they are driven out of their summer homes by December's snow and wind.

Quick ID: smaller than a robin; **Male:** gold body; dark hood; black tail and wings; bold white wing patches; yellow eyebrow stripe; **Female:** similar to male but lacks bold eyebrow and bright gold body colour.

Size: 20 cm (8 in.)

Habitat: breeds in coniferous and mixed woodlands in central and northern Ontario; overwinters sporadically in the south (irruptive).

Nest: loose bowl of sticks, twigs and plant fibres; in the crotch of a conifer or hardwood.

Food: seeds, insects (during breeding season), sunflower seeds.

Foraging: gleans vegetation and ground.

Voice: song: wandering warble; call: loud, sharp *clee-ip*.

Similar Species: American Goldfinch (p. 144) is much smaller, with black confined to the forehead.

Notes: The efficiency with which the Evening Grosbeak deshells sunflower seeds can naturally be attributed to its large conical bill. The force per unit area that this grosbeak can exert with its bill may make it the most powerful of any North American bird. • Large irruptions of Evening Grosbeaks occur every 2–3 years, with some birds going as far south as Florida. Like many other birds that overwinter in 'northern climates,' the males usually stay further north during the winter; therefore, most of the Evening Grosbeaks seen in southern Ontario during the winter are females and immatures.

House Sparrow

Passer domesticus

THIS COMMON BACKYARD BIRD often confuses novice birdwatchers because it can be very nondescript. The male is relatively conspicuous—it has a black bib, a grey cap and white lines trailing down from its mouth (as though it had spilled milk on itself)—but the best field mark for the female is that there are no distinctive field marks.

House Sparrows were introduced to North America in the 1850s, to control insects. Although these familiar birds can consume great quantities of insects, the majority of their diet is seeds, and they have become somewhat of a pest. The House Sparrow's aggressive nature usurps several native songbirds from nesting cavities, and its boldness often drives 'desirable' birds away from backyard feeders. The House Sparrow and the European Starling are now two of the most common birds in cities and farms, and are a constant reminder of human influence on natural systems.

Quick ID: large sparrow; **Male:** black throat; grey forehead; white jowls; chestnut nape; brownish-grey belly; **Female:** plain; brownish-grey belly; mottled wings.

Size: 16 cm (6 in.)

Habitat: cities, residential areas, farmyards.

Nest: bulky masses loosely woven with grass, plant fibres, synthetic fibres and twigs; on buildings and bridges and occasionally in trees.

Food: seeds, invertebrates, birdfeeder seed.

Foraging: gleans ground and vegetation.

Voice: familiar *cheep-cheep-cheep-cheep.*

Similar Species: female sparrows and finches.

Notes: The House Sparrow is a poor representative of North American sparrows, since they are only very distantly related. Most North American sparrows are not as gregarious or as aggressive as House Sparrows. House Sparrows are most closely related to the Weaver Finches, which construct elaborate hanging nests in African trees.

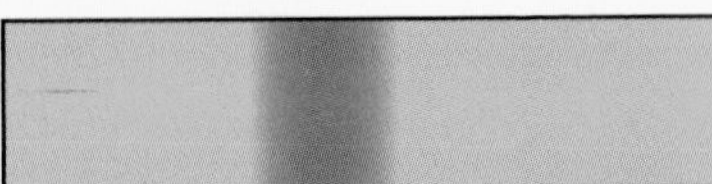

Jan Feb Mar Apr May Jun Jul Aug Sept Oct Nov Dec

WATCHING BIRDS

Identifying your first new bird can be so satisfying you just might become addicted to birdwatching. Luckily, birdwatching does not have to be expensive. It all hinges on how involved in this hobby you want to get. Setting up a simple backyard feeder is one easy way to get to know the birds sharing your neighbourhood, and some people find birdwatching to be simply a pleasant way to complement a nightly walk with the dog or a morning commute into work.

Many people enjoy going down to urban parks and feeding the wild birds that have become accustomed to humans. This activity provides people with intimate contact with urban-dwelling birds, but try to remember that bread and crackers aren't as healthy for birds as birdseed or, better yet, their natural food items.

Seasons of Birdwatching

Spring

The calendar indicates the arrival of spring about the 20th of March, but for birdwatchers the event that marks the changing of the season is the migration. By the date set according to astronomy, Great Horned Owls and Gray Jays have already nested, and Canada Geese, American Crows, and Horned Larks from the south are mingling with their overwintering counterparts. The Eastern Bluebird is a sure sign; its plumage provides a pleasant contrast to the otherwise brown landscape. Through April more migrants return, with the diversity of species mounting into the early May climax. As a cold front breaks over the Great Lakes, migrants from as far away as Argentina launch themselves from American soil over the Great Lakes. Tired by the time the first point of land is seen, the warblers, sandpipers, orioles, and others congregate on points of land to refuel for their continued flight. It is the peak birding season in Ontario, and thousands of birdwatchers have been anticipating the event. Fortunate Ontarians can avoid the crowds by birding weekdays, or by heading off to equally rich hotspots unspoiled by hordes of tourists.

As May drifts away, many birds continue north, following the shorelines and the Niagara Escarpment to northern forests where the males will sing in spring lust and nesting will begin.

Summer

The breeding time of birds comes all too quickly for birdwatchers. Summertime finds birds busy with nesting, and less likely to put on shows for human observers. Singing decreases in favour of nest-building and incubation. Once the chicks are hatched, the parent(s) are kept busy feeding the insatiable young.

For fortunate Ontarians with occupied nest boxes in their yards, summer can be extremely enjoyable. Watching the birds' reproductive cycles, from breeding to fledgling, can provide some memorable experiences. Summer closes with the young's first clumsy flight of the year.

Autumn

The fall migration through Ontario is not as focused as that of the spring, but it can be just as rewarding. Because the birds are not rushing off quickly to southern climates, the migration tends to last months as opposed to weeks. Again, geographical features funnel birds across the province with periodic concentrations gathering along the Escarpment and along the shorelines of the Great Lakes. Sewage lagoons are very productive at this time of year, but patience and expertise are frequently required as many of the shorebirds and waterfowl are not in their distinctive plumages. Migrant species disappear slowly, as their numbers gently trickle out with the coming of the cold.

Winter

Quite often southern Ontario is belted with a sudden December snowstorm that announces the arrival of winter. Winter birds are equally sudden in their appearance; the arrival of finches at the feeder proclaims the season. Although many of the grosbeaks, finches, and crossbills are variable in their pattern of occurrence, the arrival of winter usually coincides with the appearance of one or more species of these snow birds. The cold does not bring to mind images of open water, but winter is one of the best times to view waterfowl. As rafts of ducks congregate on open water (Great Lakes, cooling ponds, sewage lagoons), many species can be observed from a single vantage point.

It is also at this time of year that the birdwatcher can arrange field notes and photos, and plan upcoming trips for the spring. But take care not to overlook the overwintering birds, as their resilience and fortitude are characteristics most enviable on crisp winter mornings.

Birding Optics

Most people who are interested in birdwatching will eventually buy themselves a pair of binoculars. They help you identify key field marks such as plumage and bill colour, and also help you identify other birders! Birdwatchers are a friendly sort, and a chat among birders is all part of the experience.

You'll use your binoculars often, so selecting a good pair is important. Choose a pair that will contribute to the quality of your birdwatching experience—they don't have to be expensive. If you need help deciding which pair would be right for you, talk to other birdwatchers, or to someone at your local nature centre. Many models are available and when shopping for binoculars, it's important to keep two things in mind: weight and magnification.

One of the first things you'll notice (apart from the price extremes) is that binoculars all have two numbers associated with them, 8x40 for example. The first number, which is always the smallest, is the magnification (how large the bird will appear), while the second is the size (in millimetres) of the objective lens (the larger end). It may seem important at first to get the highest magnification possible, however a reasonable magnification of 7x or 8x is optimal for all-purpose birding, because it draws the bird's image fairly close without causing too much shaking. Some shaking happens to everyone; to overcome it, rest the binoculars against a support such as a partner's shoulder or a tree.

The size of the objective lens is really a question of birding conditions and weight. Because wider lenses (40–50 mm) will bring in more light, they are preferred for birding in low-light situations such as before sunrise or after sunset. If these aren't the conditions that you will be out in, a light pair with an objective lens diameter of less than 30 mm may be the right choice for you. Binoculars tend to become heavy after hanging around your neck all day, so compact pairs are becoming increasingly popular. If you have already purchased a pair that you are finding heavy, instead of leaving the binoculars behind you can purchase a strap that redistributes part of the weight to your shoulders and lower back to reduce the sometimes aching load.

Another valuable piece of equipment is a spotting scope. The spotting scope is very useful when viewing waterfowl, soaring raptors, or shorebirds is your goal, but it really has no use to the birdwatcher intent on viewing forest birds. A good spotting scope has a magnification of around 40x, with a sturdy tripod or a window mount for the car. (If you are looking for a second-hand model, be wary of telescopes; they are designed for viewing stars, and their magnification is too great for birds.) One of the advantages of using a scope is having the ability to see far-off birds. By setting up in one spot (or by not even leaving your car) you can observe faraway flocks that would be little more than specks in your binoculars.

With these simple pieces of equipment (none of which is truly essential) and a handy field guide, anyone can enjoy birds in their area. Many birds are difficult to see because they stay hidden in the treetops, but you can learn their songs with the many tapes and CDs that are available. After experiencing the thrill of a couple of hard-won identifications, you will find yourself taking your binoculars on walks, drives, and trips to the beach and cabin. As rewards accumulate with experience, you may find the books and photos piling up and your trips being planned just to see birds!

Birding 'by Ear'

Sometimes, bird listening can be more effective than birdwatching. The technique of birding by ear is gaining popularity, because listening for birds can be more efficient, productive, and rewarding than waiting for a visual confirmation. Birds have distinctive songs that they use to resolve territorial disputes, therefore sound is an effective way to identify species. It is particularly effective when trying to watch some of the smaller forest-dwelling birds. Their size and often indistinct plumage can make a visual search of the forest canopy frustrating. To facilitate auditory searches, catchy paraphrases are included in the descriptions of most of the birds. If the paraphrase just doesn't seem to work for you (they often are a personal thing) be creative and try to find one that fits. By spending time playing the song over in your head and fitting words to it, the voices of birds soon become as familiar as the voices of family members. Many excellent CDs and tapes are available at bookstores and wild bird stores for the songs of the birds in your area.

Keeping Bird Notes

Although most naturalists realize the usefulness of keeping accurate and concise notes of their observations, few are proud of their written records. It's easy to become overwhelmed by the excitement in the field and forget to jot down a few quick observations. It's a good idea for every level of birdwatcher to get into the habit of carrying a soft, small notebook in a large pocket or backpack. For the novice who is unsure of a bird's identity, a quick sketch (a pencil is best), and a description of the bird's behaviour and habits will help to confirm your sightings later (don't worry about your field

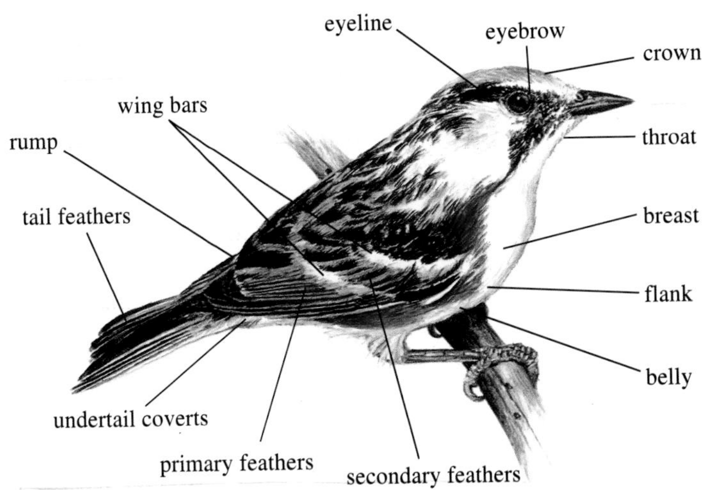

sketches—it really doesn't matter how artistic they are). For more experienced birdwatchers, dates and activities of an observed bird can be accumulated over time as an ongoing personal study. For those not wanting to bother with a notebook, a small, compact tape recorder is the easiest way to record field observations. The advantage to this method is its quickness, and its usefulness in recording unfamiliar bird calls. By recording observations and calls, your field notes can be compiled at a later time in an unhurried manner.

A notebook provides an excellent way to remember and relive the moment in the field at a later time. A comprehensive notebook can even provide information to researchers who are looking at the dynamics of birds. Even keeping a count of feeder birds over a period of years can help ornithologists with their understanding of population ecology.

Another good way to learn about birds is to join your local natural history or bird society. You will meet many knowledgeable people who will be glad to teach you what they know about birds and to show you the best places to see them. Many organizations run field trips to some of the better birdwatching spots, and they provide the benefit of an expert to help with identification problems. Christmas Bird Counts are a highlight for birdwatchers, regardless of skill level. Look for information on these in your local paper.

Birdfeeders

They're messy, can be costly, and they're sprouting up in neighbourhoods everywhere. Feeding birds has become a common pastime in residential communities all over North America. Although the concept is fairly straightforward, feeders can become quite elaborate.

The great advantage to feeding birds is that neighbourhood chickadees, jays, juncos, cardinals, and finches are enticed into regular visits. Don't expect birds to arrive at your feeder as soon as you set it up, it may take weeks for a few regulars to incorporate your yard into their daily routine. As the popularity of your feeder grows, the number of visiting birds will increase and more species will arrive. You will notice that your feeders will be busier during the winter months, when natural foods are less abundant. You can increase the odds of a good avian turnout by using a variety of feeders and seeds. When a number of birds habitually visits your yard, maintaining the food source becomes a responsibility because the birds may have begun to rely on your feeder as a regular source of food.

Larger birds tend to enjoy feeding on platforms or on the ground, while smaller birds are comfortable on hanging seed dispensers. Certain seeds tend to attract specific birds; nature centres and wild bird supply stores are the best places to ask how to attract a favourite species. It's mainly seed eaters that are attracted to backyards—some birds have no interest in feeders. Only the most committed bird-watcher will try to attract birds that are berry eaters, or in some extreme cases, scavengers!

The location of the feeder may influence the amount of business it receives from the neighbourhood birds. Because birds are wild, they are wary and are unlikely to visit an area where they may come under attack. When putting up your feeder, think like a bird. A good clear view with convenient escape routes is always appreciated. Cats like birdfeeders close to the ground, pouncing distance from a bush. Obviously, birds don't. Above all, a birdfeeder should be in view of a favourite window, where you can sit and enjoy the rewarding interaction of your appreciative feathered guests.

SELECT GLOSSARY

accipiters: genus of forests hawks, characterized by long tails, short, rounded wings; feed mostly on birds (three species in Ontario).

binomial classification: system used to give plants, fungi, and animals two names, a genus name and a species name.

biotic: term used to refer to the flora and fauna in a system.

carrion: dead animals, a food source for scavengers.

Carolinian: an ecological zone predominant in the eastern U.S. that reaches its northern limit along the north shore of Lake Erie.

conifer: cone-producing tree, usually softwood evergreen (e.g., spruce, pine, fir).

corvid: group of birds consisting of crows, jays, and ravens.

crop: an enlargement of the esophagus that serves as a storage structure and (in pigeons) has glands that produce secretions.

cryptic: colouration that blends with the environment.

dabble: foraging technique used by ducks whereby the head and neck are submerged but the body and tail remain on the water's surface.

dabbling duck: a duck that forages by dabbling, usually can walk easily on land, takes off without running, and has a brightly coloured speculum (e.g., Mallard, American Black Duck, others).

deciduous: trees that lose their broad leaves annually (e.g., oak, maple, aspen, birch).

dihedral: the position in which the wings are held in a shallow 'V' while the bird is soaring.

eclipsed: dull, female-like plumage that male ducks acquire briefly following the molting of their breeding plumage.

elbow patches: seen from below, dark spots at the bend of the outstretched wing.

flycatching: feeding behaviour whereby the bird leaves a perch to snatch insects in mid-air, and then returns to the same perch (this behaviour is also known as 'hawking' and 'sallying').

fledgling: the stage when young chicks first acquire their permanent flight feathers, but are still dependent on their parents.

flushing: a behaviour whereby frightened birds explode into flight in response to a disturbance.

gape: the size of the mouth opening.

glean: to pick small food items a little at a time.

invertebrate: animal lacking a backbone or vertebral column (e.g., insects, spiders, mollusks, worms).

irruption: sporadic mass migration of birds into non-breeding areas.

larvae: a development stage of an animal (usually invertebrate) whose body form differs from the adult form (e.g., caterpillar, maggot).

leading edge: the front edge of the wing as viewed from below.

lore: small patch between the eye and bill.

molt or molting: periodic replacement of worn-out feathers (often twice a year).

morphology: the science of form and shape.

nape: the back of the neck.

neotropical migrant: a bird that nests in Ontario, but overwinters in Central and South America.

niche: an ecological role filled by a species.

open country: an area in which the majority of the land is not forested.

parasitism: relationship between two species whereby one benefits at the expense of the other.

phylogenetic: a method of classifying birds that arranges the oldest ancestral groups prior to those that have relatively recently arisen.

pishing: making a sound to attract birds, saying 'pishhh' as loudly and as wetly as comfortable.

polygynous: mating strategy whereby one male breeds with several females.

polyandrous: mating strategy whereby one female breeds with several males.

plucking post: a perch used habitually by accipiters to pluck feathers from their prey.

raptor: a carnivorous (meat-eating) bird (e.g., eagles, hawks, falcons, owls).

rufous: rusty-red colour.

sexual dimorphism: differences between males and females of the same species (e.g., size, colour).

speculum: brightly coloured patch in the wings of many dabbling ducks.

squeaking: making a squeaking sound to attract birds, loudly kissing the back of the hand, or using a specially designed squeaky bird call.

substrate: the ground, or the muddy bottom of a wetland.

syndactyl: a foot on which two (sometimes all) of the three forward-facing toes are fused (e.g., kingfishers).

surface dips: similar to dabbling.

talons: the claws of birds of prey.

tipping up: the action of dabbling, submerging the head with the tail pointing skywards.

vertebrate: an animal having a backbone or vertebral column (e.g., fishes, amphibians, reptiles, birds, mammals).

systematist: a scientist who describes and ranks species in logical orders.

understorey: the shrub or thicket layer beneath a canopy of trees.

zygodactyl: a foot with two toes facing forward and two facing backward (e.g., Osprey, owls, and most woodpeckers).

RECOMMENDED READING

Book of North American Birds. The Reader's Digest Association Inc., Pleasantville, New York / Montreal.

Cadman, M.D, P.F.J. Eagles, and F.M. Helleiner. 1987. *Atlas of the Breeding Birds of Ontario.* University of Waterloo Press.

Goodwin, C.E. 1995. *A Bird-Finding Guide to Ontario* (revised ed.). University of Toronto Press.

McKeating, G. 1990. *Birds of Toronto.* Lone Pine Publishing, Edmonton, Canada.

McKeating, G. 1990. *Birds of Ottawa.* Lone Pine Publishing, Edmonton, Canada.

Robbins, C.S., B. Brunn, and H.S. Zim. 1966. *Birds of North America.* Golden Press, New York.

Scott, S.S. 1987. *Field Guide to the Birds of North America.* National Geographic Society, Washington, D.C.

Terres, J.K. 1982. *The Audubon Society Encyclopedia of North American Birds.* Alfred A. Knopf, New York.

BIRDING MAGAZINES

Birder's World. Holland, Michigan.

Bird Watcher's Digest. Marietta, Ohio.

Wild Bird. Irving, California.

Birds of the Wild. Markham, Ontario.

REFERENCES

American Ornithologists' Union. 1983. *Check-list of North American Birds,* 6th ed. A.O.U. Washington, D.C.

American Ornithologists' Union. 1993. Thirty-ninth supplement to the American Ornithologists' Union *Check-list of North American Birds.* Auk 110: 675-682.

American Ornithologists' Union. 1995. Fortieth supplement to the American Ornithologists' Union *Check-list of North American Birds.* Auk 112: 819-830.

Austen, M.J., M.D. Cadman, R.D. James. 1994. *Ontario Birds at Risk.* Federation of Ontario Naturalists. Don Mills, Ontario.

Book of North American Birds. The Reader's Digest Association Inc., Pleasantville, New York / Montreal.

Cadman, M.D, P.F.J. Eagles, F.M. Helleiner. 1987. *Atlas of the Breeding Birds of Ontario.* University of Waterloo Press.

Ehrlich, P.R., D.S. Dobkin, D. Wheye. 1988. *The Birder's Handbook.* Fireside, New York.

Evans, H.E. 1993. *Pioneer Naturalists: The Discovery and Naming of North American Plants and Animals.* Henry Holt and Company, New York.

Farrand, J. (ed.) 1983. *The Audubon Society Master Guide to Birding* (Vols. 1-3). Alfred A. Knopf, New York.

Godfry, W.E. 1986. *The Birds of Canada* (2nd ed.). National Museum of Natural Sciences, Ottawa.

Goodwin, C.E. 1995. *A Bird-Finding Guide to Ontario* (revised ed.). University of Toronto Press.

Gotch, A.F. 1981. *Birds-Their Latin Names Explained.* Blandford Press, Dorset, U.K.

Kastner, J. 1977. *A Species of Eternity.* Alfred A. Knopf, New York.

Mearns, B., R. Mearns. 1992. *Audubon to Xantus: the Lives of Those Commemorated in North American Bird Names.* Academic Press, San Diego.

Peck, G.K., R.D. James. 1983. *Breeding Birds of Ontario Nidology and Distribution* (Vol. 1: Nonpasserines). Royal Ontario Museum, Toronto.

Peck, G.K., and R.D. James. 1987. *Breeding Birds of Ontario Nidology and Distribution* (Vol. 2: Passerines). Royal Ontario Museum, Toronto.

Peterson, R.T. 1980. *A Field Guide to the Birds East of the Rockies,* (4th ed.). Houghton Mifflin, Boston.

Scott, S.S. 1987. *Field Guide to the Birds of North America.* National Geographic Society, Washington, D.C.

Speirs, J.M. 1985. *Birds of Ontario* (Vol. 2). Natural Heritage/Natural History Inc., Toronto.

Terres, J.K. 1995. *The Audubon Society Encyclopedia of North American Birds.* Wings Books, New York.

INDEX

Other Bestselling Lone Pine Plant Field Guides

Lone Pine's field guides have become enormously popular for their quality and ease of use. Clear species descriptions are combined with detailed drawings and excellent colour photographs to make it easy to identify everything from towering trees to minuscule mosses. Readers will appreciate the ecosystem descriptions and the illustrated glossaries and keys. With notes on the natural history, ethnobotany, edibility, potential hazards and historical uses of plants, these guides will enhance any walk in the woods and wetlands.

WETLAND PLANTS OF ONTARIO

by Al Harris, Gerry Racey and Steve Newmaster

This complete guide of wetland plants of Ontario opens up the world outside your door, with over 450 species.

• 5.5" x 8.5" • 250 pages •

• 300 colour photographs • 300 line drawings • Softcover •

$24.95 CDN **$19.95 US** ISBN 1-55105-059-5

FOREST PLANTS OF CENTRAL ONTARIO

by Brenda Chambers, Karen Legasy and Cathy V. Bentley

An indispensable guide to over 390 species of shrubs, wildflowers, grasses, ferns, mosses and lichens found in Central Ontario.

• 4.25" x 8" • 448 pages •

• 440 colour photographs • 407 line drawings • Softcover •

$24.95 CDN **$19.95 US** ISBN 1-55105-061-7

FOREST PLANTS OF NORTHEASTERN ONTARIO

by Karen Legasy and Brenda Chambers

Illustrated by Shayna Labelle-Beadman

Over 300 species of trees, shrubs, wildflowers, grasses, ferns, mosses and lichens.

• 4.25" x 8" • 352 pages •

• 300 colour photographs • 330 line drawings • Softcover •

$24.95 CDN **$19.95 US** ISBN 1-55105-064-1

Lone Pine Publishing

Edmonton Office
206, 10426-81 Avenue
Edmonton, Alberta
Canada T6E 1X5
Ph: (403) 433-9333
Fax: (403) 433-9646

Vancouver Office
202A, 1110 Seymour Street
Vancouver, British Columbia
Canada V6B 3N3
Ph: (604) 687-5555
Fax: (604) 687-5575

Washington State Office
16149 Redmond Way, #180
Redmond, Washington
USA 98052
Ph: (206) 343-9387

Phone: *1-800-661-9017*, or **Fax:** *1-800-424-7173* toll free.